2022

NEGRO ISRAELITE DAIRY
BOOK 3

yaiquab yisrael

Foreword

Anyone reading this book means that it is meant for you to read the words in this book and is for you to consider for better or worse. This is a writing solely for the purpose of documenting and testifying to the reality of the God of Abraham Isaac and Jacob. It is for the purpose of edifying and enlightening the Hebrew Israelite the Negro, the Latino, the Native American on their father's side otherwise known as the children of Israel, unknown to themselves in the current reality. It is my desire to chronicle the life I have been given from a Hebrew Israelite perspective holding back nothing of my sincerely held sentiments regarding the experiences of my captivity and my Nation as a Hebrew Israelite man to the oppressor nations currently in captivity to the white man and the people who say that they are Jews but are not of revelation 2 9 revelation 3 9. This book will most likely be of an offense to people outside of the 12 tribes or Israel or a source of rejoicing for those who are outside of the 12 tribes of Israel who can receive the truth even when it is casting the light of condemnation on them. Including my own people. The truth is many times not easy or flavorful, but it is unstoppable and forceful and will not be denied forever.

Quotes

Jesus said: Blessed are the solitary and the elect, for you shall find the kingdom; for you came forth thence and shall go there again.

Gospel of Thomas 49

"All power is Gods... how it is used is up to men"
Yaiquab Yisrael

"Have a vision. Be demanding."
—Colin Powell

Quotes

"Truth is powerful and it prevails."

—Sojourner Truth

Egyptian theology

"Nothing can produce that which it does not have in itself"

Quotes

"We all have dreams. In order to make dreams come into reality, it takes an awful lot of determination, dedication, self-discipline and effort."

—Jesse Owens, world record-setting Olympic athlete

DEDICATED TO

My mom Julia Ann Morlock

Contents

The chickens are coming home...

Hello and hello and thank you for joining me. My name is yaiquab yisrael and this is the Israelite sons of light radio program. Before I begin, I want to give thanks to my Heavenly Father earthly mother for allowing me such an incredible opportunity to be a light and a witness to the God of Abraham. Isaac and Jacob. There is no greater opportunity in the history of man, past, present, or future than to be a son or daughter of light, meaning one who is married to Messiah and their only interest is to be about our father's business.

Now, I named the title of the program tonight. "The chickens are coming home to roost". Now when you say that phrase, you really mean the skeletons are coming out of someone's closet to negatively affect them. In other words, what goes around, comes around. So, I'm going to talk a little bit about that on my radio program tonight. Now, before I begin, I want to say I am a fisher of men and women. I have a group on Facebook called the Upper room where I am looking for any Hebrew, Israelite son or daughter of light, meaning someone who realizes that Messiah is back to being the word. When he ministered to our nation. He was the Word made flesh (john 1) and when he ended his ministry, He went back to being the Word of God. Now I know that may be very difficult to receive. But that is why he says I will never leave you or forsake you. Talking to you Hebrew, Israelite Negros, Latinos and Native Americans on your father's side. You are the 12 tribes of Israel, no matter what Christianity and Catholicism says with their replacement theology you Negros, Latino, and Native Americans are the 12 tribes of Israel. In spite of the best efforts of the oppressor, nations, all those outside of the 12 tribes of Israel to steal our identity and to steal our knowledge of ourselves.

We have been revisited with the spirit of truth and are now waking up to the knowledge of ourselves and the imminent end of our captivity, to the oppressor nations those who refuse to admit who we are. Now, I want to pose a hypothetical question I forgot to say my room in for people who are married to Messiah who realize the value of redeeming the time and storing up for yourself while you are in this reality spiritually. You probably hear the oppressor nations speak a lot about prepping for the days to come. Because they realize that judgment is in the air, and they realize there is an ominous feeling hanging over them and the end of their rulership of the earth. They have written their testimony, it condemns them. They have afflicted the people of God, the Hebrew Israelites, just like it says in Deuteronomy 28 Verse 16 on, they have written the history. There is no way to change the deeds, the actions that they have done and now they are coming to the end of their blessing.

Okay, now, I want to pose a hypothetical question. If there is anyone listening to the sound of my voice, this is a hypothetical situation. Now, suppose tomorrow, the President comes on TV and says I have just received information that in four hours, we will be struck with not one not two, but three. Thermonuclear Bombs let's say thermonuclear bombs, bombs more powerful by far than what was dropped on Hiroshima and Nagasaki and in which a combined total of upwards of 250,000 people died. So, imagine the advances in technology up to the present time. Those bombs were dropped in 1945. So again, you can only imagine how powerful the weaponry that they have today. North Korea has an E M P bomb which would disable Americas electronic grid, that EMP weapon has the capability to shut down all of America's power grid Do you see how the Heavenly Father has given the oppressor nations the knowledge for the sake of destroying himself since he would not give glory, honor to the God of Abraham, Isaac and Jacob is not within him to believe in the God of Abraham, Isaac and Jacob. But I digress.

Now, the President has warned the nation that he has received intelligence that we will be struck with a thermonuclear bomb. What would you do? What would you do you Hebrew Israelites? What would anyone do? Your first thoughts I would have to say would turn to God. I perceive that anyone's first thought would be Where do I stand with the Heavenly Father? And it's a very real possibility that the President may one day suddenly get on national TV and have to give the world that message. And then the fear of the Lord would cover the earth. And then people will run to the God of Abraham, Isaac and Jacob and he says he will laugh at you. The God of Abraham, Isaac and Jacob says he will laugh at you (psalm 2) because when he called you would not come so

Behold, the seriousness of the God of Abraham, Isaac and Jacob Hebrew Israelites take the time to use your life wisely. Right now, this very second. There is a warning going out where there will be a possible God event this very month of April around the 24th. Maybe give or take one or two days and around the middle of May. Now I could be wrong. But my ministry has always been that of a family dog. Where if I perceive trouble coming real are imagined. I will start barking to warn my nation of danger. And that is what I'm doing now.

Now I want to say in the middle of all these things. Lost Is the knowledge of the Hebrew Israelites, the children of God, the Hebrew Israelite Negro, Latino and Native Americans the world knows not who we are does not care. And even to this day, America and its police officers continue to gun down Hebrew Israelites denying them justice using them as window dressing. Lost in all the confluence of events are the Hebrew Israelites. I pray that I am reaching someone who desires to leave the world behind and to join me in my room on Facebook, so that we may start to redeem the time together. Okay, now the chickens are coming home to roost. America has a history of going in other countries for the sake of their gold and any other resources they deem valuable. Now you can ask Venezuela Iran, Libya, Brazil and now you can even ask Russia.

If John chapter 10 Verse 10 is true about the thief only coming to kill steal and destroy. America fits that bill. We now are at the end of our rope because economically the dollar cannot survive because it is not backed by anything. And we are now making excuses against Russia to start a conflagration. blaming them for chemical weapons, unproven, the same way they did to Iraq. We are doing the same to Russia and that is a precursor to invading another country and the beginning of hostilities. The Russian president has said if that happens, he will use nuclear weapons the Russian president has warned he will use nuclear weapons. Now to draw you Hebrew Israelites. You Hebrew Israelites attention to First Thessalonians five I have been mentioning this many times in my past videos for the sake of comforting you where it says we meaning, the children of Israel are not appointed to wrath. We meaning, the 12 tribes are not appointed to wrath. So let us forsake what we see in the world. And let us draw nearer to the God of

Abraham, Isaac and Jacob. The chickens are coming home to roost for America for its history of corruption and because of the way they have treated the Negro not African Americans, not Africans, but the Negroes.

The chickens are coming home to roost. Are you ready? To stand before the son of man are you ready to give an answer for the reality that he has given all of us the chickens are coming home to roost for our oppressor nations. The events in the world today are Reaching a fever pitch there is more talk of the virus coming back there is a cry for more laws which will take away more freedoms. As a country we claim to want to get to the bottom of things. But one of the chickens that is coming home to roost is the power hypocrisy of America. America is being exposed now. For the hypocrisy of saying one thing and doing another the corruption of our political leaders is being exposed. There has been a lot of talk, which many of our Hebrew Israelite nation knows nothing about concerning the current administration and influence peddling and how the political observers and researchers are discovering information on paper that will condemn most of those in power right now. You must understand, I cannot be to detailed because we are under censorship.

I want to say that the reason for my ministry is to sound a warning for you Hebrew, Israelite sons of light I do not deceive myself into thinking I will reach hundreds of people. But if you can hear my voice, please consider that this word is for you. Your life is a vapor. You will not hear this message for much longer. The scripture says wrath is not appointed to our people. The scripture says the 12 tribes of Israel will be saved out of Jacob's trouble (Jeremiah 30 7). That means since any day now hostilities can begin. We must be removed before the wrath of God sets in. Now, I have also been talking about 2024 And the final slant of the x that crosses America. So, if my overstanding is correct, it means we must leave before 2024 For you Hebrew Israelite sons and daughters of light should consider that very deeply. Do not be taken away with the pull of the world. The desire for riches and the dainties of this life. I mentioned a couple of weeks ago overnight Germany raised its prices from 20% to 50%. They raised their food prices. It is Revelation six three coming to life, this is the finger of our God, the God of Abraham, Isaac and Jacob the oppressor nations. They sense that the life they always knew has come to an end and many times I look on videos and see people are getting religious suddenly. And even still, they refuse to admit who the Hebrew Israelite 12 tribes are. Even to this day, they do not know who we are.

Brethren, please let me say to you store up treasure that faded not away reserved for you. Join me in my room on Facebook called the Upper room where we will try to minister to you to help you write your testimony in the Earth using digital words so that they will follow you all your life and let us help you to endure this reality. Let us help to encourage you to continue and overcome the world. And this darkness, there is a great darkness there is no knowledge of the God of Abraham, Isaac, and Jacob. We live under great agendas of transgenderism of feminism, all kinds of depopulation agendas. This is the Heavenly Father warning you now is the time flee from Babylon. Join me please consider joining me for ministry and for fellowship you brethren who are married to Messiah, you need to join with other brethren who speak your language who are waiting for their life to be counted worthy to stand before the Son of Man.

 I want to give thanks to my Heavenly Father earthly mother for this incredible opportunity. Please join me Wednesday and Friday 8pm Pacific Standard Time and until I see you again. May peace be unto you

shalom

a shame

some people
I hate to say it
But it's the truth
Then again

I don't hate the truth

But then again
maybe I do
Because
this type of truth

I don't like
But you know what?

Somebody's gotta say it
This world
Has a lot of people
Who kill your faith

Or at least
Try to

And that really sucks

People who can only see
Themselves
Narcissistic in spirit
You must needs feed

Either there
Stomach
Their wallet
Or ego

For nothing in
Return
These people

Kill your faith in God

Always needy
Always seeking
What they can get
From you

But

Looking at the TV
How come everyone
Seems
to come across

As the total opposite?

Of what I know
To be true?

You start out young
Totally opposite
Of what eventually
You become

A god damn
Con artist

Look at
Little children
Willing to share
No ego

Anywhere
to be found

very virtuous
All their young life

But as they grow
They know not God

And then become
The people I see now

hands stretched out
Nothing they give back
Never wondering why
They always lack

And there stands
Most powerful God

Creation spread out

Always giving
In abundance and goodness
Man gives no thanks
But he takes and takes

Two hands stretched out
One to take
The other you to give
Selfishness and greed

To kill your faith
Making you believe
God is that way
We live to take

But we love to receive

People kill faith
Grabbing at life
Getting what they can get
And in the end

Nothing to receive

ABRAHAM ISAAC AND JACOB

To the Hebrew Israelite, sons of light radio program. It is a ministry that I have for the sole purpose of fishing for men of the Hebrew Israelite nation, sons and daughters of light, people who are who are able to realize the purpose of their reality and to take advantage of the contest in the world, as it says, In the Book of the Nag Hammadi scriptures, the gospel of Philip, the Heavenly Father states that he has placed a contest in the world to see who his sons and daughters are. I have a website for ministry information, you can go there in order to get in contact me. If the things I say resonate with you.

Okay, I wanted to name the title of the program tonight. Abraham, Isaac, and Jacob. Recently, I was sitting around doing nothing when I began to meditate. And something that came to my mind was the fact that the name of the God of Abraham, Isaac and Jacob is pretty much forgotten in our nation because of the explosion of information. It seems to have blessed us and made us forget, at the same time, the God of Abraham, Isaac, and Jacob. You know, it's interesting, when you are anointed to be married to Messiah. He takes away the world thoroughly in your mind, if you are married to Messiah, a lot of the things that happen in earthly relationships are analogous to the reality of Messiah. In other words, the things that take place in an earthly marriage can also be attributed to the reality of the God of Abraham, Isaac, and Jacob. It's really interesting, the way people know about the God of Abraham, Isaac, and Jacob, but the pull of the world has taken away their ability to manifestly go about their reality. Storing up or redeeming the time. This is a reality where the requirements of living force you to put aside the spiritual truth, for the sake of helping you to store up and redeem the time, I like to talk about the successful people in the world. Later in life, after years of labor, suddenly, they begin to reap the fruits of their labor.

People must work in anonymously, obscurely studying, going to school staying up most of the night to research and to learn the things of this world. And then after 12 or so, years of school, meaning college, they begin to reap the fruits of their labor. It is the same way when you are married to Messiah you must learn to sacrifice it least even a little. Me being a fisher of men, and a son of light, am thoroughly amazed at the lack of reaction. The word of the Messiah gets. The word is Messiah. He was the Word made flesh, according to John chapter one. But since we are tied to the flesh, only a lively stone son or daughter of light can see Messiah in the Word. He was the word made flesh but, now Messiah is in Word for and we cannot see him for the most part, meaning those who are not anointed to be married to Messiah that shows you the effect the flesh has on our mindset.

Now let me say when you look at people in the world, you observe the world in a way, most people cannot. I should have said when you are married to Messiah, you tend to look at people to learn a lesson and their lack of spirituality. To let it be a warning to you. And you also tend to observe the world in a way most people cannot, about all things. The Bible says a spiritual man judges all things.

By looking at the things of the world, you see the glory of God in everything. You witness, the God of Abraham, Isaac, and Jacob in all things even the most minor of things. When you are married to the God of Abraham, Isaac, and Jacob, it means you also want to manifest this belief in your life. Imagine you are married to a woman do you think you will get away with ignoring her? There will come a time. I guarantee you. The day will come where she says she wants to break up with you, the few times in my life that I have went through that were devastating. Especially when you see her with her new boyfriend. It is one of the most devastating experiences that life will let you see. The effect it had on me was to stay away from relationships. There is a saying "once burned twice shy" when you are burned once you become twice shy. another thing that I have seen and my reality is thoroughly broken people, especially of the female principal it seems that I have only been meaning spiritually emotionally broken people of the world not just my nation, people with psychological problems, emotional problems, spiritual problems. I have been hearing stories incredible stories of damnation and destruction that have happened to people in their life. And I have also noticed another thing.

The lack of testimony of the God of Abraham, Isaac, and Jacob. In addition, people are thoroughly, totally oblivious to their spiritual self so that they cannot minister to themself spiritually. The Heavenly Father said draw near to Him and He will draw near to you. One of the mysteries of the female principal is the energy that you give to her. She will give double back to you. That is one of the great mysteries of the female principle. Another thing that I have seen in my reality is the opposite of what happens in the female principle. There is an incredible lack of mindset agreement. There is a total lack of unity in marriages that I have seen where people are unequally yoked spiritually. And to me, it makes me shake my head that this is the case. People start out everything is lovely. And as the years go by, and they teach each other more, one is spiritual and the other is not and that is like living in prison. As far as I am concerned. I remember those days and finding out that the women that I felt I wanted to marry, I could not join myself to them because they were tied to the earth. And when I realized that it left a permanent scar on my soul because there is nothing a son or daughter of light can do when you are in that situation, when that realization comes to you, you can attribute those days to days of woe and depression and anxiety.

You are torn between two kingdoms, the earthly and the spiritual. I cannot imagine anything worse. Drawing on experience of living with someone that lives in a different kingdom then you live in. I cannot imagine anything worse. And there are so many broken people in the world. That alone tells you that we do not know the kingdom of the God of Abraham, Isaac, and Jacob.

Sometimes I hear people say a lot I would die for my country and it always intrigues me because I would rather live for the God of Abraham, Isaac, and Jacob. I want life not death. In this reality, people play around with reality of life after death. The

Edomites the white man, he plays around with the reality of life after death. He has a different outlook on the reality of life after death and what happens? He says in this reality, I will die for my country and why he has that mindset in a nation that claims to be a Christian nation. is totally beyond my overstanding. Judgment is a reality that this world likes to keep from acknowledging men has proven that he cannot judge himself. He cannot govern himself. That is one of the reasons we were given our reality.

Again, I want to mention something I read in the Gospel of Phillip. The Heavenly Father placed a contest in the world to see who his sons and daughters are meaning, who would in spite of all the vicissitudes of life still gravitate to him. Like a cat coming home after it was lost in a faraway country, say like from Florida to California. It somehow finds its way back home, is that not the most amazing thing? The Heavenly Father has placed a contest in the world to see who his sons and daughters are Hebrew, Israelite, Negro, Latino, Native Americans. The Heavenly Father placed a contest in the world to see who despite all the oppression affliction and vexation that this life gives to you Hebrew Israelites who will in spite of all those things still make their way home to the Heavenly Father. That is what Messiah came for, to show us the color of the Spirit and how we should think and how we should act. I like to mention that we are all works in progress. We will not worship perfectly but when you are married to Messiah, you will certainly show an effort to the world who your heavenly Father is and what you are in this life. Now, when I was saying earlier, that people who are successful they work in obscurity for the early part of their life. They give themselves over to rigorous training and learning in order to later prosper after all, the years of learning and study and repetition, and application is no different than the Hebrew Israelite sons and daughters of light. So far as the effort we should put forth, for the God of Abraham, Isaac and Jacob. The effort is paramount to the Heavenly Father.

Currently, he has made it very easy to show effort. It simply means to find ways to reach out to other Hebrew Israelites and minister to them. Any little thing is commendable to the God of Abraham, Isaac, and Jacob. Some people minister more consistently than others. Most of ministering and being Married to Messiah involve your spiritual mindset and application of the things you learn. You can worship the God of Abraham, Isaac and Jacob by reading, acquiring over standing and worshiping, spiritually that way. You're your actions speak volumes and this reality. I want to say that we are living in a time where trumpets are blowing. But these are trumpets that we cannot hear. These are the types of trumpets that are silent. These trumpets give warning. Now, recently, I was talking about APR 24 2022. And the fact that there may be a move of God in our reality. I heard a commentator say we may be witnessing the third seal of revelation being open. It has to do with death and financial reset. The third seal of Revelation. It is blowing very loudly. The Heavenly Father is warning that this may be a move of God. In the next few days of the month of April

I learned something that was interesting the other day. And you 2008 There was a financial crash. I remember seeing the movie. "Too Big to Fail". And it was based on what really happened in the year 2008. It was the year of the financial crash. And there was a part in the movie where the person playing Ben Bernanke was speaking. Ben Bernanke was the head of the Federal Reserve. He was speaking, he told one of the movers and shakers who oversaw the banking industry. He said Mr. President if you don't do something Monday morning, you will not have any economy, now keep this in mind. From 2008 Or I should say up to the year 2008. It took America what 100 years to create $100 trillion 100 dollars years. Do you know that in the 2008 financial crash, they had to come up with 7 trillion in a couple of days? And that was the life support that kept the economy going even until today. And we have no way of paying that back. We are under threat that the dollar may no longer be the reserve currency for the world, because Saudi Arabia as I mentioned in a previous video seeks to have a renewed military alliance with Russia. Which spells doom for the American dollar because now they are considering using the ruble which is backed by gold as the new reserve currency. Our money is not backed by anything. Do you want 100% of nothing or 1% of something? We are in perilous times. Absolutely.

I want to give thanks to my heavenly Father, earthly mother for this totally incredible opportunity. I want to say join me Wednesday and Friday 8pm Pacific Standard Time, go to my website 12 tribes israelites.com for ministry and information and until I see you again.

Peace be until you

shalom

first vibrations

when you first find out
What it's all about
the first vibrations
Of a spiritual walk

The call to come
On the road
To the Kingdom
The call of God

Those first vibrations
I don't know when
But I could not resist
The first vibrations

When you feel something
In your soul
No knowledge of how or why
You must follow

Not knowing where to go
The first vibrations
Carrying you along
Until you hit your stride

Onward you go
Letting the patience
Helping you to grow
The God of Abraham Isaac and Jacob
In full control

A vision in your mind
The angels by your side
A whisper in your heart
It says from this road do not depart

The color of life
The good and evil

So that I might
Choose rightly

For my eternal good

The first vibrations
When you think and wonder
About the reality of God
Of Abraham Isaac and Jacob

And you consider
The things you do not see
But they are there
Just a little further out

The other side
of reality

When you hit your stride
And the first vibrations
Began to subside
As life takes shape

You have become a veteran
In running the race
Filled with humility
And Thanksgiving

Because of
Your many blessings
Hindsight
2020

Everything starts
With first vibrations
Asking you to come
To a world

Unseen as of now

The offer still stands
As long as
You recognize
The Kingdom is within

ZERO HOUR

Thanks for joining me. This is yaiquab ban yisrael. And this is the Israelite, sons of light radio program. I want to thank you for joining me. I want to give thanks to my Heavenly Father and my earthly mother for this incredible, incredible opportunity to be a light while I am in this reality, if anything I say resonates with you then please go to my website twelvetribesisraelite.com where you can get in touch with me for ministry and information. I just have published a new book where you can check it out on Amazon. You type in my name yaiquab ban yisrael, and it should come up and it gives you a little option to check it out. It's basically me writing my testimony. While I am in this reality, something I tried to highly encourage anyone to do. Use the present time somehow to put your reality down on paper or either digitally or whatever way you can think of to be a witness for what you want to do, according to the desires of your heart so far. As testifying about the God of Abraham, Isaac, and Jacob.

Okay, now, I previously said something on one of my videos, and I want to correct what I said because it was wrong. I mentioned that up until the year of 2008. It took America 100 years, I said to create $100 trillion what I should have said is that it took America 100 years to create $1 trillion now in the 2008, financial crash on one weekend, we created $7 trillion dollars to save the banking institution, up until the year 2008. We created $1 trillion dollars. But in one weekend, we created $7 trillion in the 2008 financial crash in order to save the banks. Okay.

So that gives you an idea of the fact that we are living on borrowed time. America needs a new revenue stream. They need resources. That is why we have been going in to other countries and fulfilling John Chapter 10 10. The thief cometh not but to kill, steal, or destroy. I want to mention that the title of my radio program tonight is "zero hour". We are in a time right now. That the reality as we have known it may soon come to an end. Let me go back for a second and conclude my thoughts on the financial situation. Because it has a lot to do with the title of my program, the creation of the amount of money that previously we had not created until after 100 years the fact that we printed so much in just a few days. Let's you know we are on borrowed time you Hebrew Israelite sons and daughters of light. This gives you a picture of why America is fulfilling John chapter 10 verse 10, going into other countries and taking their resources and even taking their gold. As of recently Russia was sanctioned. And they have been seizing the yachts of people called the oligarchs, the elite of Russian society in order to put pressure on President Putin. We are on borrowed time, we cannot nearly pay back the money that was printed in 2008 to save the banking institution, the other nations know this. So therefore, we must go to war with Russia and go after their resources, just like we did with Libya, Iraq and tried to do with Iran Venezuela parts of South Africa John chapter 10 Verse 10. America has left a trail of bloodshed and death. This is the picture of borrowed time. Now, zero hour means time has run out. I again want to remind anyone who is listening about the 24th of April, only a couple of days from now. Now I may be wrong the scripture says despise not prophesy. I have been wrong before. But I will not stop warning anyone of my nation who will listen about what I perceive to be danger, great danger coming to this nation I want to say something before I go on about something I noticed recently in the confluence of events. I have noticed that recently, America likes to include an Israelite face on the different evil agendas that they do. I recently took note of the fact that they used Colin Powell as the face of the Iraqi invasion, remember, weapons of mass destruction? only to be found out to be a lie. Remember, Lloyd Austin? the Secretary of Defense, mightily doing the will of the white man's military agenda. And now they have appointed an Israelite woman to the Supreme Court to uphold the laws of our oppressor nations? There is a pattern where the oppressor nations like to put an Israelite face on the evil that they do. So, like little children who get caught with their hand in the cookie jar. They immediately tell on their brother too and say, what about him? as if that will save them from the judgment to come. They put an Israelite face on the agendas that they do. That is the reality where we live brethren. But now, we are in zero hour where like it says in Revelation 18 17, In one hour in one hour. Babylon's great riches come to nothing. It has to happen sometime. The scriptures say it will happen suddenly. We have been taken away with the distractions of the world.

Even our nation, taken away with the dainties of this life. Always thinking tomorrow will come not knowing the reason for your existence in the present reality which is to show that you are a son or daughter of light, that is the only reason for the existence of a son or daughter of light who worships the God of Abraham, Isaac and Jacob. We are witnessing more fulfilled prophecy in this day. We are witnessing severe infighting between the Edomites mainly manifested through Republicans and Democrats scheming against each other for power. The acrimony between these two parties has reached a lethal level. I have been looking at certain videos about the election, the presidential election and the claims of President Trump that the election was rigged. The videos that I have been seeing are very conclusive, of election fraud. Now me personally, I could not give a damn about the election. But I seem to see the Heavenly Father working to destabilize our oppressors.

The oppressor nations. The evidence is conclusive that the election was stolen. When you see videos of people putting bags of votes in mailboxes at night on closed circuit cameras, catching them in the act. There should be no doubt in anyone's mind of the corruption in our government right now. There is so much corruption. It can only be because the spirit has left this country a long time ago and has returned to the Hebrew Israelites who are waking up knowing who we are. Knowing who we were knowing that the kingdom of God is ours and right now, there is a mental affliction on the oppressor nations because they remember their history of how they have treated us and it is causing a mental illness in them because they know now you are in zero hour where we will come out of our bondage and captivity and we will rule over you because the time of your gift of rulership of the Earth has come to an end.
Now, when I look at what's going on, between Russia and Ukraine, I am a human being and I do not like to see suffering and death and bloodshed all over the place. When I see the videos of people being shot at close range, I do not want to be in a reality that is like that. It is the Heavenly Father showing us what happens when men do not worship the God of Abraham, Isaac, and Jacob. No one in their right mind wants to be a part of that reality. Our prayers have gone up. The Heavenly Father has heard them and the confluence of events are showing us that we have come to zero hour no more time left for us to be in captivity to our oppressor nations.

I call to mind the eclipses. I call to mind the planet Pluto incredible revelations to give comfort to the Hebrew Israelites to let us know to look up because our redemption draweth nigh ,2024 the X across America. Can anyone deny this must be the finger of God the Heavenly Father. Can anyone deny the supernatural manifestation of the X across

America in 2024 Brethren when you read the scriptures in First Thessalonians 5 it says that we you lively stone sons and daughters of light shall not be appointed to wrath the scriptures talk of our sudden deliverance when the portals of the earth open up and we go in to them. If my understanding is correct. Brethren, if we are awakened if we are witnessing the things that are going on right now. It should cheer your heart it should bless your soul. The Heavenly Father has struck the oppressor nations with a mental illness that is so devastating that at a time where they should sincerely acknowledge the truth. At a time when the oppressor nations should diligently inquire into the children of Israel, so that they may turn and receive some type of crumb of mercy. They still cannot acknowledge who the children of God are, so that they might turn and try to do good unto them. I am constantly witnessing videos where Christian pastors love to talk about how glad they are that they are believers.

They say nothing about the Negro. The Latino or Native American. They only can think of themselves even at a time like this. Where the confluence of events gives a mighty warning. The kolbrin Bible speaks of the destroyer. I recently saw videos, plural videos of the reappearance of the destroyer, cycles after cycles of time the destroyer makes its appearance. Now some people may call it Nibiru or Planet X. In my best overstanding, it is the same thing. Brethren, the point of everything I am saying is we live in a nation where death and where tribulation is imminent.

Brethren, we live in a nation that is in its final demise. Now is the time for any Hebrew Israelite under the sound of my voice to run for your life, from Babylon, from the dainties of Babylon from the distractions of Babylon I want to call to mind something I witnessed with my own eyes about Revelation six. I live in the Bay area of California, in South San Francisco. And from time to time, I go across the bay bridge where you can see ships coming in and out to deliver their containers or to leave to go get more, and I have seen with my own eyes, ships outside of their ports, a multitude of ships maybe 30 or 40 of them that cannot deliver their goods. I have heard of this same thing in Los Angeles. How for some reason, containers are unable to deliver their product. I have also been hearing of food shortages in the stores. I have been hearing of rising prices. I have heard about in one night. Germany, food prices rose from 20 to 50% overnight. Brethren in America is not a nation prepared to do without fast food or life's luxuries. I want to say to you Hebrew Israelite sons and daughters of light, it will go well with you and we have nothing to fear. The only type of prepping that we should be doing is drawing nearer to our father and to be about his business as we watch our oppressors meet their final end which is now, the third seal Monday next week, it may come to pass where there is death and a reset of the financial institution. The third seal of Revelation as far as I can tell, the information that I had seen may very well be anointed. It will be a shock to the whole world. What the Heavenly Father may have planned for this reality when suddenly like it says in Corinthians, that we shall be changed. When you look at the oppressor nations I have to say again, the look on their face when they see who the Israelites are, to me is worth all of the years that the oppressor nations have afflicted me afflicted my nation just to see the look on their face when the Heavenly Father reveals who the children of Israel are, to me, that will be the greatest satisfaction that I have ever witnessed in my life. That is what keeps me going to minister to know that the Heavenly Father's Word is truth and it will come to pass that you can be sure of.

 I want to give thanks to my Heavenly Father earthly mother for this incredible opportunity. If anything, I say resonates with you and you believe you're married to Messiah join me in my room on Facebook, called the upper room until I see you again Wednesday or Friday. 8pm May peace be unto you,

Shalom

QUICKSAND

Hello and thank you for joining me my name is yaiquab ban Yisrael, and this is the Israelites sons Light radio program. I want to give thanks to my Heavenly Father earthly mother for this opportunity to be a light to be about my Father's business while I am this reality, if anything I say resonates with you. During the course of my program, please go to twelvetribesisraelites.com for ministry and information I just published a new book. You can get the information at the website twelvetribes israelights.com If you're interested in reading about the things I like to share with our nation, the Hebrew Israelites, the people of Negro, Latino and Native American lineage on their father's side okay.

 Tonight, I named the title of the program, "quicksand pt4". If you have been listening to my radio programs over the past few weeks, I have been talking about nothing but quicksand. And I did a video on April the 19th and previously speaking about April 24. I did a video called" zero hour" and I warned of an event and I was wrong in my expectation, but right in the fact that there was any event and it made all the sense in the world to me. If I were to ask anyone listening to me, what was the event that happened on the 24 and the information even went out at around midnight, American time. If I were to ask anyone, under the sound of my voice, what do you think that event was? There may be two or three of our nation who knows what I am talking about. I am speaking of the fact that the nation of the people of revelation two nine and Revelation three nine starting with a J and ending with an s ditched the dollar our good friends over there in the Middle East. Ditched the dollar and none of you heard about why? Because the mainstream media does not want America to know that they stabbed you in the back and you know nothing about it. They ditched the dollar. Does anyone know what that means? That means we must find a way to restore the dollar because other nations are no longer doing business trading with the dollar especially for Saudi Arabian oil. If you are paying attention to the confluence of events, you will see the BRICS nations Brazil, Russia, India, China, South Africa, lining up against Babylon and its dollar world government, too. Bring it to its end, as it says in Revelation 18 in one hour. Now, again, the third seal of Revelation the horsemen with the scale and his hand. The seal has been opened. There was an event on the 24th It started out under the radar, as if when you light a fire first it kindles and then before long it turns into a raging fire most of us do not know what happened on the 24th. The event that I had been speaking about was a match being lit. And now all we must do is wait for the kindling to be turned into a fire. That's where we are at right now.

If you look at Revelation chapter six, and the third seal you will notice something very, very interesting that I learned about just today. Ukraine is a majority producer, a leading producer of exactly the items that it mentions. You guessed it, Revelation chapter six. Those of you who are familiar with Revelation chapter six, it talks about the items that our soon to be greatly decreased in our time resulting in food shortages. And if I'm not mistaken it mentions in Revelation chapter 6 oil which is what Ukraine is a leading producer of and it also mentioned wheat, which the Ukraine is a leading a leading producing country of, but it says hurt not the oil and the wine. Now I thought it was interesting that I should say Revelation Chapter Six is the chapter I am speaking of where it speaks of the horsemen and the warning about the food shortages and the scales, meaning the financial reset. Now the scripture says and when he had opened the third seal, I heard the third beast say come and see. And I beheld and lo a black horse, now Black Horse meaning death. And he that sat on him had a pair of balances in his hand. And I heard a voice in the midst of the four beasts say, "a measure of wheat for a penny and three measures of barley for a penny and see thou hurt not the oil and the wine". Now, two of those products are very interesting. The wheat and the barley and the country of Ukraine is a leading producer of these things. Now we have been witnessing if you're following the news again, attacks on food processing plants.

The effect of these attacks will resonate as we go on in this year, they will be greatly increased because of the hostilities in Russia and Ukraine and the loss of the crop that is produced by the nation of Ukraine and Russia for that matter. So, what we have here is a perfect storm for the decreased exports of barley and wheat and even oil. The three things that are mentioned in the third seal of Revelation are produced by the countries currently at hostilities with each other. So, the farming will not be able to produce what it has been producing in a previous years. Now, the effect of the current events so far as the food shortages do not happen overnight. And in this you should be able to see the God of Abraham, Isaac and Jacob slowly bringing about a massive fire on different fronts that will totally catch all the world off guard except for the Hebrew Israelites if you listen to the churches, the Christians, they continue to tell their people that they are looking at the possible rapture of the church. They look at their white Messiah as warning them they are getting ready to leave this reality. They have more information, meaning the oppressor nations about the secret things that are going on in the present reality and the agendas and it is quite interesting that they are fulfilling Psalm chapter 64 where the heavenly father, the God of Abraham, Isaac and Jacob is making their own tongue fall upon them. Meaning the contacts that they have sharing with the world. The secret things we will not hear in the mainstream media.

Again, I want to go back to what happened on April 24. Revelation two nine revelation three nine those people have turned their back on the American dollar. You heard nothing of it in the mainstream news. I follow the events of the things that fly under the radar so that I may run and tell my nation, there are plenty of financial economic analysts if you will just go online and go to different social platforms who are warning of a financial collapse in accordance with Revelation chapter six. That is why the scripture says in Revelation chapter one every I shall see Him because He will be behind this collapse. He says he comes suddenly he says he comes as a thief in the night. Now personally, I was disappointed that there was not a great explosion in the world. And to be honest, I was disappointed that our nation was not taken away. Although I knew that that would not be the case. I do know that the Hebrew Israelites will receive the gold and the silver of the world. Just like what happened in Egypt when they borrowed of the Egyptians. precious items and the scripture says they plundered the Egyptians. We are witnessing the lead up to the same thing that happened in Egypt getting ready to happen again, where somehow, we will plunder the Egyptians again. And to that I look forward to, as I know the rest of our nation does.

I want to say something that I thought about a couple of days ago that you may find interesting. Now if you count from the last financial crash from 2008 to 2022 that gives you 15 years and for some reason. I began to think of the account in second Kings and the account of Nebuchadnezzar when he was informed that he was soon to die. And it says he turned his face to the wall and began to plead for more time.

Remember in Second Kings and he was granted 15 more years. Now, I may be wrong. But it seems like America had been granted 15 more years at the end of the crash of 2008. So, 2008 plus 15 years brings us to 2022 exactly the year that many financial analysts are predicting the mother of all economic collapses. You should be able to see it if you are looking and studying what is going on. And if you can put two and two together you will clearly see number one, we have food shortages. Number two, we have the threat of war and rumors of war. Number three, we see the dollar and the financial reset that many of the powers that be already taking shape even as I am speaking to you, Russia and other nations have already dumped the dollar there was a military alliance made between Russia and Saudi Arabia. Erasing the petrol dollar because Saudi Arabia will now accept oil in other currencies. The petrol dollar anyone will tell you is the main staple of the American economy.

When you look at the God of Abraham, Isaac and Jacob the warning he gives is unheeded. Historically, that has been the case with the prophets with Noah warning the people and even till today the warning is going out. But the urgency is not there. For our nation for many of our people to draw near to the God of Abraham, Isaac, and Jacob.

And let me say something interesting that I forgot to say in my previous videos since I found out do you know the word Hallelujah means praise not yah? Haven't people been saying that word for decades. Hallelujah. Do you know that means praise not yah? The correct way for praising the father is HALALYAH that is the correct pronunciation when we want to say praise God halalyah, But I digress. I want to call to mind the current situation concerning Revelation chapter six. It is a time of great quicksand where the world is caught in the agendas of the elite. There is nothing they can do about it. They see great judgment on the horizon. alliances are being formed between the West meaning Europe and the United States and the East meaning Russia and China primarily we should be able to see those things clearly now. I read an article in the newspaper the other day about how now the colleges and universities are speaking of making reparations to the 12 tribes' descendants who have built the prestigious colleges and universities of the nation. And Harvard University wants to pay the grand total of $100 million. Isn't that just swell? $100 million dollars as payment for probably billions of dollars that Harvard has made since its inception. Watching the mind of the oppressor nation in this day and age has been a real study in mental illness. And I know is the affliction of the God of Abraham, Isaac and Jacob. They will not recognize the Hebrew Israelites. They only know their own pain and suffering. They will not discuss the ethnicity of the Bible. They cling even more firmly to the white Messiah for is as advanced as this world is in its technology. In its so-called silence and the artificial intelligence that it is creating when it comes to the obvious who the children of Israel are. They are as dumb as a brick. Brothers and sisters, I want to say to you draw nearer to the God of Abraham, Isaac and Jacob. I have a room on face book. I am a fisher of men and women. I want to help you to redeem the time by simply writing digitally your testimony while you are in the earth. Send me a friend request on Facebook. And if you believe you are married to Messiah then please join us in our room. You should clearly be able to see the demise of this place that we call America. We are done here. We are finished here. We see that one day we will wake up and we will go to the store and they will say we no longer accept dollar bills. The fact that Israel dumped the dollar speaks volumes mainly because you will find them and control the world finances through their central banks. So, if they move away from the dollar, then brethren, we have now entered quicksand where it is just a matter of a short period of time. From the time that whatever is in the pipeline of the supply chain runs out and the nations of the world trade in their own currencies. Second, that we will feel the effects of hyper-inflation, loss of our bank accounts. And the scripture will be fulfilled where people will run to the God of Abraham, Isaac and Jacob seconds and he says he will laugh at you because when he called you would not come meaning today right now. Figure out ways where you can redeem the time. Maybe even possibly find a way to minister to other Hebrew Israelite brethren. The fact that most brethren or sisters have no works built up will cause a severe affliction in your own mind. And no one wants that for you

I want to give thanks to my Heavenly Father earthly mother for this incredible opportunity. I want to say join me Wednesday and Friday and until I see you again, please be into you

Shalom

QUICKSAND PT 3

I talk about the situation surrounding the Hebrew Israelites today on my radio program, I only talk about three or four things only always, remember a movie I saw called "school ties" and at the end of the movie, the person who played the character of a Jewish school boy football player which the school had conspired against him. Because they did not like the fact that he was Jewish. At the end of the movie. Brendan Fraser says to Matt Damon No, I'm never going to let you forget who I am. This was after Matt Damon said to him after he had been kicked out of school and was in a car on his way home. This is what he said," you will still always be a god damn. Jew "and then Brendan Fraser replied with and you will always be a such and such. It is the same way in our reality today. The memory of the children of the God of Abraham, Isaac, and Jacob is the one thing that the oppressor nations want to do away with more than anything because the sight of the Hebrew Israelites constantly reminds the oppressor nations of the slave trade the actions of the evil that was done to the Hebrew Israelites and this is a stain that they cannot remove. The Heavenly Father has not given them the ability to recompense us to forget about us to give justice to us at this moment. And so, every time they look at us, the memory comes back over and repeatedly.

And since we are presently under the curse, there is nothing they can do to assist us to lift us up or to prosper in this present reality. Now, like I said earlier, I talked about only three or four things. I talk about the redemption of the Hebrew Israelites. I talk about the inheritance of Hebrew Israelites. I talk about the coming captivity of the oppressor nations, those nations that have enslaved us, that have put us into hard labor and have not recompensed us who have killed us, even to this day. Those are the things that I like to talk about on my broadcast or my ministry. I write books. I am in the middle of my seventh book. You only need to buy one book to know what is in the other books. Because as I said, I only write about the same thing, different ways as a testimony to the God of Abraham, Isaac, and Jacob. Because in this reality we have reached a time where there is no mention of the God of Abraham, Isaac, and Jacob. There is no pointing to him to our nation. As the God of all mankind. There is no knowledge of the God of Abraham, Isaac, and Jacob the flood of information has made the oppressor nations… and sadly, our nation as well has made people forget to give glory to the God of Abraham, Isaac, and Jacob. Those are the only things that I pretty much talk about. Now, that's the way I see it. No one must believe the way I do. Right now, we have different brethren in the nation of Israel. And most of them are light brethren. Brethren who minister to you, and they minister in their gift. They Minister according to what wisdom, knowledge and understanding they have. It's as simple as that. One brother may have a gift of the pseudepigraph books, the mystery books, you may have a gift of reading the stars another brother, may have the gift, of the historical, Hebrew Israelites. All these brothers have been given to the 12 tribes. of Israel to minister to them. It is an incredible opportunity to spend your life storing up for yourself. Redeeming the time. These brothers who are ministering to the nation of Israel are storing up and redeeming the time. They have been elected to walk a path most of us are not able to. It is the highest calling that any of us can ever hope to attain. But you must be elected to be this type of son or daughter of light, who is able to spend the majority of their time ministering at their own resources and out of their own resources consistently to the nation of Israel. Now I have a room on Facebook for very special people. And I am a fisher of men and I am looking for Hebrew Israelite sons and daughters of light to simply join us and to spend the reality you are under to write your testimony in the earth. I'm not saying you have to join me in order to write your testimony in the earth. But it is certainly a very very great opportunity to put your faith and reality down in digital worlds. That's what my room is for. This room this fellowship is for brethren who can respond to the word as it goes out. Brethren who feel they can participate on a semi regular basis now, just send me a friend invite and let me talk to you to see if you will be able to benefit from my room because most people who come in are not able to produce fruit. After a couple of days. They become stillborn where they will not participate. They will not bear fruit; they have not had the over standing that the word is Messiah. So, I want to warn anyone listening to the sound of my voice.

Now, I want to say this. We live in a world where the oppressor nations just want us to forget who we are. They want us to forget our memory. They don't want us to talk about the evil of slavery or the other things they have done that they know must come into judgment. They do not want the Hebrew Israelites to raise their voice to tell the truth or to go out over the airwaves. When you look at the past few years, it seems like maybe in the 70s or even earlier in the 60s, the term went out. We found out who we are. We ran with it. It grew it was a very popular subject on social media. It was getting many views from brethren who were on the street, telling the nation and telling our nation who the Israelites were and that we had woken up. And part of that waking up is the knowledge that we will recompense those who have afflicted us and that is what the nations of the world tremble at. Because when your family has been afflicted for 200 years, and really even more because that's what it says in Genesis 15 13. The slavery called chattel slavery came to an end. But slavery as an institution did not come to an end. Now, very simply put, if you go from 1619 The start of the Mid Atlantic slave trade to 2019 That is exactly when the confluence of events things we have never seen before began to come on the earth. I am talking about the vaccines. I'm talking about the hostilities presently going on. I am talking about the knowledge of the planet Pluto making its re-appearance in the skies. beginning its ending cycle of 249 years I believe, meaning the end of Pluto cycle will end in 2024. And it coincides with the solar eclipse seven years from the first one where the solar eclipse will cross the sky opposite of the way the first eclipse Prost America back in 2017. Brethren 20 24 x across America, it means the end X marks the end at least as far as I can overstand it marks the end of Hebrew Israelite captivity. Now I could be wrong. But I know that it means a very significant move of the Heavenly Father for the good have the 12 tribes. Hebrew Israelites the nation of Israel, you Negros, Latinos and Native Americans. Now when you look at the world the conspiracy is clear of the nations against us. The other nations conspire against Israel conspire meaning when people do things without your knowledge and you do not see it until the action is manifested. A conspiracy against the Hebrew Israelite sons and daughters of light is being committed at this very moment. And the Edomites and those who say they are jews are guilty of conspiracy. The Edomites meaning the Caucasian man and the revelation two nine revelation three nine people they know that they are under a judgement.

Now judgment is not a very popular topic in this reality. That's why I was saying earlier. We are in a situation where the oppressor nation wants to wipe our memory clean. We look at the oppressor nations commercials. And we see Hebrew Israelites as happy as they could be dancing and doing a jig for the white man. And that is just the way they would have it. Ignorant Hebrew Israelites who do not like the truth.

They don't want you to talk to them, even families of Hebrew. Israelites don't want to hear about who we are, who the 12 tribes are. When you start to walk in the light. Remember, you are surrounded by darkness, even your own family when you begin to walk in the light, you are learning the afflictions of Messiah and you must endure you must walk to the end of your life beginning, ending where you started, that is the mystery of life. Now, I want to mention again, how the oppressor nations do not like us to remind them of who we are. And in this day and age, it is working tremendously as most of our nation does not tell the oppressor nations of the judgment to come for them and that we have not forgot.

Now, I called in to a radio station called kgo a couple of days ago, and I knew I was not going to get on the air. And the host went on. He belongs to the revelation two nine revelation three nine of the tribe of those who say they are jews. I hope you can decipher what I am saying. I called in to his radio program, knowing that he would not let me on and an hour and a half later on the John Rothman Kgo radio program. I still did not get on. Most likely because he knew that when I heard him mention national Holocaust Remembrance Day that I was going to call in and say that's funny because it's also national Mid Atlantic slave trade day. But they would not let me on. I have a second phone, which I did not use at the time. I will wait to a later date to call in and make a tremendous point hoping that our people will hear it.

now I am saying this because you brethren can do the same thing. You can do the same thing. You can call in to different talk shows and look for an opportunity to inject the knowledge of who Messiah is who the Hebrew Israelites are. And if enough of us call various radio stations and find a way to inject the knowledge of the Hebrew Israelites in the God of Abraham, Isaac and Jacob. Then it must at some point become a news item. When I call in. They can simply ignore me. But they cannot ignore 100,000 Hebrew Israelites saying the same thing, warning the world that we are the 12 tribes and judgment is a reality and it will come to pass. It will have to come become a national news story about multitudes of people calling in to the John Rothman radio program and other radio station programs across the world to let them know we are the children of Israel. There must be a recompense for the evil that has been committed. The time is now and so on and so forth. The oppressor nations would not be able to stop the spread of that type of information going out if a multitude of you brothers and sisters take the opportunity to get the word out and the fact of who we are. And what is going on right now is the beginning of Revelation chapter six. The black horse with the rider and the scales and the prophecy of the barley and the oil such as (sunflower seed oil and canola oil) and the wheat which I mentioned the other day are three of the key products that Russia and the Ukraine export to the world. How do you like that? and there it is mentioned in Revelation chapter six, the prophecy of the rider on the black horse and the scales in his hand, one day's wages for a quart of wheat and three pennies for the Barley. And hurt not the oil and wine, now the oil is being hurt because they cannot export oil or harvest the amounts they have previously because they are in hostilities, one with another. You see the prophecy of the third seal being open. And just recently, the president threw $33 billion at the war but when it comes to reparations, well, you know, we can't afford it right now. That is too much money. But when their buddies in the Ukraine come crying with their hands stretched out, what do they do? Right away? They go and dig into our pockets. Yes, the Hebrew Israelites and they hand over cash. You see the hypocrisy of America. You see how we live in a hypocritical nation and world you Hebrew Israelite sons of light, Negro Latinos and Native Americans. On your father's side? Do you see the hypocrisy? Do you see the quicksand that we are currently witnessing all around us? I read an article just recently where the President of Russia threatened nuclear war and he does not mean he is speaking idly. President Putin has shown that he will use forces military forces to quell a situation like he did with the Chechen uprising a few years ago, where he warned them, he warned him and then he went in and blasted them even though women and children were there. America is in a situation where they must destroy themselves.

Okay, until I see you in Wednesday and Friday 8pm Pacific Standard Time. I want to give thanks to my Heavenly Father earthly mother for this incredible opportunity and until I see you again peace be unto you. Halalyah

Shalom.

Quicksand pt. 4

So, thank you for joining me. My name is yaiquab ban Israel. And this is the Israelite, sons of light radio program that I like to try to do. Every Wednesday and Friday at 8pm Pacific time. I want to give thanks to my Heavenly Father earthly mother for this incredible opportunity to be a light while I am in this reality if you have heard my previous radio programs, my only desire is to glorify the God of Abraham, Isaac, and Jacob. That is the whole reason for my existence. In this day and age. Can you tell me the last time you've heard someone mentioned, the God of Abraham, Isaac, and Jacob? That is done on purpose to put you to sleep, so that you will just drift away? That is the desire of the strange woman of Proverbs chapter five she wants to kill the children of the God of Abraham, Isaac and Jacob Lilith. And one of her methods is to distract you either with pleasure or with pain or to appeal to your desires just so long as you stay away from glorifying the God of Abraham, Isaac, and Jacob.

Now before I begin, I have a couple of items that I'd like to share with you. I have been trying to share recently that in our nation, it is very popular to say hallelujah, when we want to praise the God of Abraham, Isaac and Jacob. Don't you know that that we're actually means praise? Not yah. Halleluiah means praise, not yah. When we want to praise God, the God of Abraham, Isaac and Jacob we should be saying halalyah which means praise God. Doesn't that sound like Satan? Where he removes a couple of letters in order to throw you off. But we are in a day and age right now. Where little by little brick by brick. We are coming in to our truth of the oppressor nations and the knowledge of our kingdom. For the Negro, Latino and Native American and any other person, no matter what tribe or nation willing to submit to the truth of the Word of God. That's a beautiful thing. The problem is that we live in a world of people who are so proud they will never admit to the fact that the Negro, Latino and Native Americans are the children of Israel. People are willing to suffer eternal chastisement rather than admit that the people that you have afflicted all these years, the people that have provided a good living for you, given you luxury and abundance those people, the children of Israel you will not acknowledge as the 12 tribes of the God of Abraham, Isaac and Jacob that is truly a shame.

Okay, I also want to ask any of you that is listening to my radio program, I am going to start making an appeal that you call your local radio talk show program and educate them to the knowledge of the fact that we are not black people. That we are the children of Israel and the knowledge of the God of Abraham, Isaac and Jacob. Now, I know what you are saying in your mind's eye right now. Which is good luck trying to call a local radio station talk station to educate the public on the 12 tribes of Israel. And you are right. You will get absolutely nowhere you will be cut off in one and a half. seconds. I know because I try to frequently call in to kgo radio in the Bay Area. Whenever I listen to a talk show The John Rothman program on kgo Whenever there is a subject matter where I can jump in and interject the Hebrew Israelites, and the God of Abraham, Isaac and Jacob and the reality of the fact that we are the people of God and in exactly 10 and a half seconds later I will be listening to a dial tone. The radio station out here has Jewish talk shows in order to implement their agenda daily. And I imagined it is that way across the nation where the revelation two nine, revelation three nine people will not allow the knowledge of the God of Abraham, Isaac and Jacob to go out over the airwaves. So, my only hope is that you would try to witness that way to your local radio station and be a light and use your energy that way. Okay. And also, I forgot to add if you want to get a good idea of the quicksand of the darkness even more than what you already know. Try to do any kind of ministry and you will see that you will quickly be put on an island meaning by yourself and that will be the Heavenly Father. Testing, testing you and that is the will of the Father to try every son and daughter of light to see who will be able to endure their life and give a witness of the God of Abraham, Isaac and Jacob. And it is to you people who gained the victory that the greatest riches the father has to offer will go to you. That is what life is all about. Will we endure our life? Will we still gravitate to the Heavenly Father in spite of all the daily events that Vex you that oppress you? That make you mad? Or it makes you glad. Everything is meant to test you. If you read the Kolbrin Bible, it will tell you the purpose of Mother Earth. The purpose of Mother Earth is to hand you over to the Heavenly Father. The purpose of Mother Earth is to grow you up and make you ready to turn you over to the God of Abraham, Isaac and Jacob so that you may engage in greater works for the purpose of the expanding kingdom of the God of Abraham, Isaac and Jacob. That is the purpose of this whole reality. Now I want to share something that bothered me greatly. And I mean, greatly. I do not know why. For some reason, it came upon by spirit out of the blue out of nowhere. The thought popped in my mind. Watch a video of a nuclear attack simulation,

now before I elaborate, I want to say I don't believe I am like a lot of other Hebrew Israelites who have dreams and they have visions. I am not like that. I cannot really testify of an anointed experience. Like that. Like you hear other people say. So maybe I do experience these things, but I just don't know. But I thought this unction was quite unique to me to look at a simulation of a nuclear war and my mind was blown by what I saw. Brethren I beg you go to YouTube, type in nuclear war simulation. And believe me, you will fear the God of Abraham, Isaac and Jacob you will start to examine yourself and where you are in the faith. You will look at life very differently after having seen that video, it made me think about what is the most important thing in this reality by far and that is to redeem the time and to store up and to only work for the God of Abraham, Isaac, and Jacob. Believe me, that will be your only thought, we live in a world where nobody knows the God of Abraham, Isaac, and Jacob. We live in a world of quicksand. Where we are slowly being degraded where we are slowly sinking in our existence, so far as economically, so far as the end of life, as we have always known it. This is a world that is coming to its final end, having nothing to show for the God of Abraham, Isaac and Jacob. What I mean is having nothing to show so far as works of faith in the truth. Christianity has been a major player in all these things. When you look at that nuclear simulation, interestingly, it is not the falling explosion of bombs that does the most damage when you look at that nuclear simulation, it will be clear to you the most damage comes from Fallout nuclear radiation fallout. The bombs will explode. The winds will carry the radiation all over the world to the point where the earth will be covered with radiation. Brethren I beg you to look at that video and use it to increase your faith the fallout from a nuclear weapon is called nuclear winter and if you have been listening to the Russian precedent it is easy for him now to warn that he will use nuclear tactical weapons and if there is any interference from foreign powers. He wants to make it clear that he will use not only nuclear weapons, but weapons we have not seen before. That is the day and age that we are living in. And the Edomites are begging for nuclear war because they want to see what it will be like. I want to say to you Hebrew Israelites. There is a great warning on the horizon. Now is the time that we want to use our energy and whatever way to be a light and to use our energy whatever way we can think of to write our testimony in the earth for the God of Abraham, Isaac and Jacob

Okay, I also want to say I am a fisher of men and women who believe they are married to Messiah. I am begging you to join me in a room I have on Facebook called the upper room where basically I try to keep you encouraged on a daily basis with scriptural snippets for you to read and meditate on during the course of the day. So that hopefully, you will be able to minister one way or another while we are in this reality. That is the will of the Father to seek and search for that. Which was lost. That is the children of Israel. So please, if you can send me a friend invite on Facebook. And hopefully let me get a chance to talk to you about the room and also to warn that this is the type of ministry that requires you to participate. It is a very dangerous thing to have the word of the light of the Heavenly Father go out and you cannot respond to it. You don't want to join a room like mine where eventually you become stillborn. You cannot respond to the word not even once in a month. So, make sure before you contact me that you count the cost of being a part of a ministry such as the one, I have. Now, another boiling pot issue that is on the world stage. That is most likely the reason why the confluence of events are what they are is the fact that the dollar is close to being insolvent. If you have been paying attention, you will notice that other nations are now starting to back their currency by gold. If you are following the confluence of events, you will realize that Saudi Arabia for one is trading their oil and other currencies. All of this points to the demise of the dollar. So, in my humble opinion, this suggests that unless we find ways of going into someone else's country, like America is famous for and stealing their resources to prop up our dollar then we are doomed. And the other nations know that we are on borrowed time. I mentioned a warning about the 24th of April. It seemed to come and go with no event at all. But on that very day. We're it got out that Israel. ditched the dollar Israel ditch the dollar. Our old buddy stabbed us in the back. Billions and billions of dollars we gave in support of that nation. And they ditched the dollar. That means they will trade in other currencies. Now we tend not to pay much attention to that. But brethren, what it means is that we have lost a trading partner. We have found a way to lose a currency stream which in turn will dry up the pipeline that we previously had when we were trading with Israel. Brethren, we are now existing on the things that are already in the supply chain. But we are realizing when the supply chain runs out, then we will understand the significance of these many nations that are no longer using the dollar to do business in internationally. In addition to these things, do you know the French president has announced an ID card that will control their citizens buying and selling and the same for Australia New Zealand and even Italy. They have ID cards that they are implementing that will control your buying and selling. And yet you never hear about these sorts of things in the mainstream news because do you know that recently, a Ministry of Truth was created to subdue dissenting opinions. Do you see the nature of America to spite the truth? Brethren I want to give thanks to my Heavenly Father earthly mother for this incredible opportunity. Join me Wednesday and Friday 8pm Pacific Standard Time and until I see you again Shalom.

Shoot the negro

When things
Don't go your way
Shoot the negro
I heard Payton Gendron say

When demons come
Your spirit overrun
Shoot the negro
I heard Dylan roof say

If an excuse you need
To hide your shortcomings
Shoot the negro
Shoot the negro

Shoot more than one
Shoot more than 6
For that matter
Get as many as you can get

You will get off
If you claim
Psychological insanity
Everyone will forgive you

Shoot the negro
And the Jews will say
Holocaust Holocaust
All over again

Never mind
11 people lay dead
Never let a good tragedy
Go to waste

When you are tired
When you are vexed
The Negro

An easy target

When blood
You want to shed
Because you need
Someone to blame

Why not shoot a negro?
Revenging power
He has none
No provider no protector

Totally subjected
To the will
Of the oppressor

The children
Of the Most High God
Broken in sorrow
In heart and mind

Because of the judgment
Because of the curse
Because of Deuteronomy
chapter 28

It is the word of the Lord

So, when you feel down
And feeling blue
And your tree lined Street
And manicured lawns
In the suburbs

Not enough for you
or of sufficient breast milk
You were deprived
Or
You are tired of being white

Shoot the negro
To ease your mind
Knowing that
The evil you spread

Will give Satan much delight
Lord and master of your soul
And hell
Your eternal abode

Safely secure
In the nether world
And all killers of the children of Israel
And murderers and thieves
Of the negro to go

Quicksand 5

Okay, I wanted to name the title of the program tonight. quicksand. Number five. Recently I've been doing segments on the confluence of events and the present reality, the things that have been happening since 2019 are no coincidence. What so ever. If you are like me, a Hebrew Israelite son, or daughter of light, you should know by now that an anointing has been done to you to cause you to think about spiritual things. You should know by now, even if you are a younger, Israelite meaning a negro, Latino or Native American you should know that you are special that you are anointed and that you are gifted because you tend to think on spiritual things. Because you tend to focus on the God of Abraham, Isaac, and Jacob because you look at the world you live in. It is hard for you to find someone to have fellowship with to talk about what really matters in life. To talk about ultimate reality, which is the eternal kingdom of God. It is hard for you to fellowship and share the things you are learning the things that bless your soul. It is hard for you to try to bless someone else's soul with the knowledge of the God of Abraham, Isaac, and Jacob.

But still, you find it within your spirit to continue and to endure the present unbelief. And let me tell you, the darkness is ever thickening. In the present reality because of the confluence of events with the virus with the opening of the seals of revelation with the current hostilities in Russia and Ukraine. And there are many things that our nation the Hebrew Israelites that we do not know is going on right beneath our nose because you are too tied up in this reality to look for the things that the mainstream media will not tell you. That is one of the reasons for my ministry. That is why I am a fisher of men and women, I prayed to be in the situation I am in. I am afflicted. I am disabled. My body is wasting away. But my inward man is being renewed day by day. And that should be your testimony as well. Last week, I did not do my radio shows because I was afflicted again by the evil one, which caused me to stay in the hospital for a week. Anyone who desires to live godly in Messiah will suffer persecution. Anyone who desires to redeem the time and to store up treasure will suffer persecution. Let me say this again. When you read the Kolbrin Bible, one of the things that it tells you is that you sons and daughters of light, are not here in this reality, to live it up. And get all you can get and be as popular as you can be. And to live in the lap of luxury, all your life, like the world says you should live. The Kolbrin Bible says if you go even six months without some sort of affliction, or vexation, you are fortunate above most people,

You Hebrew Israelites, sons and daughters of light. Let me say to you, messages like this are on the way out. You will not hear messages like this. Speaking about the God of Abraham, Isaac and Jacob, and the opportunity we have, in the current reality, to overcome the world, to bear fruit unto Our Father who art in heaven. By way of being a light to our nation. messages such as this one and the messages of like- minded brethren, will no longer be heard. I say this because of what it says in Revelation, where the voice of the bride and the voice of the bridegroom will no longer be heard anymore. And I have to believe we are on the very brink of this message being silenced once and for all. Because the day of the Lord is at hand. The warning has gone out. It is mainly unheeded; the Saints have been worn out what it says in Daniel chapter seven. We have no strength left to pray, to meditate. to commune with the angels. What we are told to do in the Essene gospel of peace book four, we have no strength because the majority of us are just trying to survive the present evil all around us. Now let me digress for a second. Yet another mass shooting was committed a couple of days ago by some suburban white kid who decided it would be a good idea to drive a couple hours away just so that he could mow down some Israelite brethren and sisters simply because he's not satisfied with the direction of the country and mass immigration and the decline of the Caucasian race. So, what better opportunity to take it out on the Negro when you're feeling down when you're kind of blue. Just go out and shoot a negro. Nothing will happen to you. The police may even buy you fast food in the patrol car. Like they did that demon named Dylan Roof in South Carolina then he shot up that church. Hell, then you might only even get probation even though you kill eleven. Hebrew Israelites. Can anyone under the sound of my voice over stand? Why it is my prayer daily that Babylon fall speedily? Now when you look at the seals of Revelation, it talks about the souls under the altar who steadily make request how long how long? Oh, Lord, Faithful and True. Dost thou not avenge our blood shed upon the earth? When you read that it should let you know. The God of Abraham, Isaac and Jacob is going to take vengeance on our oppressors. That is a message that the oppressor Christian Catholic nations like to forget about. The love doctrine is fit within the Israelite nation and has taken captive. Many of our brothers and sisters but I digress.

When you consider what happened in Buffalo and the mass shooting it is a result of some something I was speaking on a couple of weeks ago on a previous program. The danger that we as the Hebrew Israelites face on a daily basis is the fact that we are a living reminder to the oppressor nations that there is a bill that they must pay. There is a bill that has to be paid before we can be good buddies with one another. There must be a recompense first. Then we can be all the buddies you want to be, but that slate has got to be wiped clean first. And that is why from time to time. Some edomite will flip a switch in his head when he sees the Hebrew and he knows subconsciously what has been done to us and what must be done to them. Just as the Word of God in Ezekiel chapter 25. Starting in verse 14, we are a living reminder to the oppressor, nations that the God of Abraham, Isaac and Jacob has not forgotten us and we are now in a time where any point the confluence of events in the world today must surely know the 3rd seal of Revelation is being open right now. It is so unmistakable even though I have been reading and studying it and re studying it and reading it. Over and over again I cannot stop my mind from being amazed at the clarity of the seals being open. Meaning the white horse, the red horse. Now in my over standing I could be wrong. But I believe the seals have to do with America and Europe and Russia and China and I also believe the beasts spoken of in the book of Daniel is a prophecy about America and the European Union and how the beasts for wings were which I perceive is America raising up the European Union, but the prophecy says the wings of the first beasts will be clipped. That means America. Babylon will be cut off and the European Union will be on its own to deal with

Russia who will be told to arise and devour much flesh now that America is out of the way it makes all the sense in the world to me. And I' seem to recall that America disappears from prophecy at some point. Now, in my humble opinion, I believe that is speaking of America being hit with an EMP weapon. It used to be one of my favorite topics years ago when I was heavy into prophecy, and I first found out about an EMP weapon and how it will knock out the electronic grid of the whole country if it is detonated in our atmosphere.

I recently heard a message of a political prognosticator speculating that if America is hit with an EMP weapon, which we most likely probably will be, we will not be able to defend ourselves. We will not be able to fire back on the perpetrator. We will be a sitting duck in the water. Now, these are things you are not going to hear about in the main stream media. These are things that you must pray and ask for revelation about and there is an anointing on many of the things that are being brought out in social media today that our Holy Spirit Inspired. If you look for Messiah, you will find him if you search for him. You Hebrew Israelite sons and daughters of light. The bride stays up looking for Messiah and he appears to her he encourages her. He says he knows that you feel all alone, that no one wants to hear what you have to say. How no one wants to glorify the God of Abraham, Isaac and Jacob with you. He knows that he sees that, but it must be that way for you sons and daughters of light. We must overcome this reality. We must endure. We will endure. Only look at the works that the Heavenly Father is doing for us right now. He is fighting for us. Those people over in the Ukraine and Russia. They don't look like us. That is the Heavenly Father making them fight and kill each other and it will spread we must go to war with Russia because of the De dollarization of the dollar and how oil and other commodities are being traded. In other currencies other than the dollar. That means we must go to war because war is profit for America. Brethren the reports about the food shortages are real. I recently saw a video where there are 1000s of shipping containers, lined up outside of various ports of China. Brethren I've said that correctly 1000s of containers that have not been delivered and if you think about it, those containers if they are not offloaded, they cannot be reloaded in order to engage in trade and commerce to bring supplies that are needed. I recently read an article where India has just recently nationalized its wheat, meaning they are not going to engage in trade and selling it because they need it. I read an article about a 10% reduction in the rice crop which more than likely will be upwards of 20 or 30% reduction because of the lack of fertilizer and herbicides that the farmers need to get a harvest so that they may ship and trade with the known world. These are undercurrents that we do not see that are in the pipeline, but we will surely be affected. I spoke about April 24. I was hoping for an explosion but what happened was even more ominous and nobody knows about it, Israel our buddy, Israel ditched the dollar. when you have an ally turning their back on you like that. That should tell you your days are numbered. Brethren I have a room on Facebook. I am a fisher of men.

Now is the time to redeem the time. That's my whole purpose of ministry. To look for anyone who wants to redeem the time and store up treasure and write your testimony in the earth because you are in a world where no one cares about their spiritual foundation and we are approaching a time where all you will have left to stand on are the things that you do to draw nearer to the God of Abraham, Isaac and Jacob now is the time to get busy.

Please contact me on Facebook. My room is called the Upper Room. Send me a friend invite and let's store up the time and redeem the time together

I want to give thanks to my Heavenly Father earthly mother for this incredible opportunity. Join me Wednesday and Friday 8pm pacific standard time until I see you again.

Peace be unto you

shalom

I feel like someone my age should not be asking questions such as this, is this world really real? Are the reports I hear of pedophilia among the elite and powerful and prominent in this current reality for real? Up till now I have turned my ears away because of the unbelief that people really commit such things against the children of the earth. But it seems as if every day I am bombarded with reports of pedophilia globally and child trafficking among the most powerful people in our society. Is this really real what I am hearing about pedophilia? Are people really so bold as to commit such crimes against the most helpless individuals of our society? Are people really really so bold as to commit these crimes before the face of the God of Abraham Isaac and Jacob? I am only now beginning to except the fact that people are afflicted with this sickness of pedophilia. I have been hearing of rituals of child sacrifice and other abominable acts that I cannot bring myself to mention in this book. Up till now I have closed my ears to such talk refusing to believe that this sort of thing really happens. But as I grow older, I am realizing that people really are capable of committing not only this type of atrocity but other acts of darkness that I perceive many of us do not have a clue about. Truly at the present we live in a bloodthirsty greedy lustful world of spirits of men devoid of the fear of the God of Abraham Isaac and Jacob.

People such as myself who fear God greatly are vexed out of our wits end. It reminds me of the scripture where it speaks of lot vexed with the deeds of the wicked. As I witness these things it drives me further and further away from the course of the world. I even find myself giving thanks to my heavenly father that my parents do not have to live anymore in a world that is so evil and corrupt and full of murder and killing it seems everywhere I look. It plagues my mind how anyone would not seek to sow to their spiritual self, knowing the temporariness of the reality that we live in. Many times, it seems that this reality is a living nightmare especially when I think of the disregard of the truth and the secret agendas of a few evil people under the power of the gods of this world and how they can affect the lives of so many people to make them miserable with their inventions and evil schemes.

I used to think that these organizations were totally committed to the welfare and brotherhood of man because of their global influence. But now I see that any organization needs money to exist and therefore are made subject to the source of revenue that sustains their existence. Enter people like Bill Gates and Klaus Schwab and other sources of unlimited money to buy off the organizations that claim to serve men but really do not. They serve agendas and those agendas usually have one bottom line and that is dominion and control of the world. I continue to be amazed at how long it has taken me to finally come to this conclusion. It is increasingly evident that the gods of this world want to make this a godless society totally devoid of any knowledge of the God of Abraham Isaac and Jacob. The message of Matthew chapter 4 keeps coming back where Satan offered the kingdoms of the world to Messiah if only Messiah would fall down and worship him. The kingdoms of the world are being brought to worship Satan if not already. I ask again is this all really real and the answer is yes, it is really real.

quicksand 6

this is the Israelite sons of light radio program that Heavenly Father willing. I try to do every Wednesday and Friday at 8pm Pacific Standard Time. This is a program where I try to fish for Hebrew Israelite sons and daughters of light people of Negro, Latino or Native American lineage on your father's side. I forgot to say, I want to give thanks to my Heavenly Father earthly mother for this incredible opportunity. That I have to take my life and to be about the business of the God of Abraham, Isaac, and Jacob. Every moment I am alive, I have a website where if the things I say resonate with you, you can contact me at twelvetribesisraelites.com for ministry and information I write books. I have the room on Facebook, all of which you can find out about on my website, twelvetribesisraelites.com And I want to stress again, in this day and age easily, anyone who is spiritually minded should be able to see that if you are about the business of the God of Abraham, Isaac and Jacob, easily, that is the greatest, highest blessing you can be under.

Now, I wanted to name the title of my program tonight. quicksand. Number six. Recently, I have been doing a series on the confluence of events, signaling the end of Israelite captivity and I want to start off with a little story about a conversation that I had with my neighbor and in talking to my neighbor, about the current hostilities in the Russia Ukraine area. I made a statement to him that all injustice will be recompensed and he agreed with me. But when the conversation turned towards the injustice of the oppressor nations, to the children of Israel, he didn't agree with what I was saying, because he was condemned. So, no logic that I shared with him. No argument I made no matter how persuasive could convince him that all injustice would be recompense. He refuses to believe and even the most basic logic behind my argument. And it occurred to me this is the mindset of the oppressor nations. They see that they are condemned and their own justice system demands a recompense for every crime committed. But when they are condemned, they refuse to believe there should be any recompense concerning their history of abuse of the children of Israel. They refuse to believe that they should be recompensed for the evil that has been done. And I thought to myself, this is really amazing. This is a form of mental illness; the oppressor nations are under right this very minute.

Now, I also want to say this, because I came under criticism from someone whether of our nation or not, who said, Israelites are just as wicked as the oppressor, nations are and I agreed, I was upset because it seems I hear more often from people who are critical of my radio program than those who support me. That is the power of negative energy. When someone has an opportunity, it seems to criticize, then, more likely than not, they will. But that is neither here nor there. He did have a point. Our nation seems to be just as evil as the oppressor nations when we go about killing, our own kind, robbing, raping and stealing from our own nation. We recently I observed in the news, they have been pointing out taking great pains to show the world that Israelites can be just as evil as those who oppress us, focusing on the events in Chicago and the incredible wickedness that is going on there. It seems as if the oppressor nation wants to say to the world, see, they are as evil as we are. And I believe that they do things like focusing on our nation because of the embarrassing events such as the recent cases of Armaud Arbury Breonna Taylor, George Floyd, the buffalo shooting Dylan Roof and it seems as if they want to even the score every time and Israelite fires a gun. They seem to want to feature that 10 times more than the atrocity their own people commit against us. As if the wickedness that Israelites do will negate the fact that their judgment will somehow be less than it is a form of mental illness. In addition to all the other problems going on, in our oppressor nation, and this reality.

Before I begin, I want to testify to you sons and daughters of light, something that is heavy on my soul. But I know without a shadow of a doubt what I am getting ready to tell you is the truth. It is true. Many of our brethren are not preparing a solid foundation of works and faith and prayer and meditation while we have the time. Do not let this discourage you from enduring the present unbelief. Search your heart search your mind to be a light some kind of way to our nation. Work on your foundation of faith. Read study learn, support other brethren who are laboring to try to feed you the word to help you to endure your reality. For the many brethren in our nation, they have problems of their own, too. But these brothers and sisters are anointed to help us to focus on the God of Abraham, Isaac, and Jacob. Because if you have been paying attention, the world has long forgotten about the God of the Hebrew Israelites. Brethren, if anyone is listening to me, this one thing I know is true. That if you work to build your foundation, and your faith in your wall, and your works, you will find rest unto your soul that the whole world is looking for. Let me repeat for any son and daughter of light of the Hebrew Israelite nation, if rest for your spirit is what you are looking for. If rest is what you are looking for in your soul, search yourself. Examine yourself. Imagine ways that you can be about the business of the God of Abraham, Isaac and Jacob which is basically ministering to your nation. One way or another. Do not give 100% of your energy to the oppressor nations do not give all of your energy just trying to survive and hold on to a reality that is only temporary.

If you set your heart and mind and soul to seek and draw nearer to the God of Abraham, Isaac and Jacob through prayer through ministry through worship and supplication, whatever way you can. You will find rest unto your soul. Now, I have written six books. I am in the middle of my seventh book. My writings are not very good. If you ask me. I do not have a high opinion. Scholarly speaking that is of the things I have written. But I could not be happier that I have written six books and am well on my way to finishing my seventh book. Because it is my testimony. It comforts my soul when I want to sleep at night. I want to bless my soul knowing that they have been written. No one can take them away from me no one can make me deny them. They are works that will follow me among other ministries and works that I have. It gives my soul rest many times before I go to bed. I have my books lined up where I can see them. And I give thanks until I fall asleep knowing that I have written my testimony about the God of Abraham, Isaac and Jacob while I had time while I was in this reality and I want to say to anyone listening to me, there is no greater feeling, no greater feeling knowing that you have labored to be a light knowing the eternal cosmic blessing you are under, you sons and daughters of light are under knowing you can redeem your family and friends according to pistis Sophia, chapter 128, when you go to sleep at night, and you can look back on things you have done and are doing to glorify the God of Abraham, Isaac, and Jacob. You will find rest on to your soul. Of that I can guarantee is true.

It will nurse your soul as you think in your mind about the things that you are doing in this reality to build your foundation, so that when the time comes for us to give an account we can do so with assurance whenever you build your foundation if you are looking at the current reality, you see very few people attempting to build a foundation to the God of Abraham Isaac and Jacob. Jeremiah 3 14 "I will take you one of a city and to have a family". That is the rarity of a son or daughter of light who can somehow find a way to be about your father's business in the current reality.

That is what my room on Facebook for to help you to write your testimony to build your foundation so that it will witness what you were about while you are in this reality. The angels record the things we do and make a report to the Heavenly Father every evening. Did you know that? Do you know who the communing angel is right now during the daytime? What about the communing angel for Monday during the daytime or Tuesday or Wednesday or Thursday? Or what about the communing angels during the evening during the week? I'm pretty sure you know when the Sabbath is Friday Evening, Saturday evening, which is the worship of the Father. Do you know when we are supposed to greet the earthly mother? These are things I tried to help you remember in my room on Facebook. Come and join me and my brethren so I may try to help you stay focused and bear fruit while we are in this reality. I want to say something about the current situation in the world that we most likely know nothing about.

Does anyone realize that at the end of the month Israel and the United States will conduct a military operation called War Games simulating an attack on Iran? at the end of this month has anyone been watching the stock market crashing lately? Is it any coincidence that after the damage has been done, all of a sudden, they're thinking about outlawing abortion? Does anyone know that Finland and Sweden are seeking admittance into NATO and what that means? Do you know the threat that the President of Russia has made if they join NATO?

One thing I know in my soul is the God of Abraham, Isaac and Jacob is moving on our behalf. One thing I know in my soul is that the God of Abraham, Isaac and Jacob is going to pay America back for slavery. For racism, for raping and robbing the children of Israel for bombing other nations for destabilizing other nations for war mongering for its political corruption for blaspheming, the children of Israel and the word of God America will be repaid by the God of Abraham, Isaac and Jacob for the over 400 broken treaties with the natives for its corrupt morality, for its transgenderism, bisexualism lesbianism transhumanism for abortion for its Christianity for its Catholicism for its colonialism for its present day depopulation agenda for its corrupt in the economy, business practices for the oppression of the Hebrew widow and children, for the police brutality for its white Messiah for living deliciously at the expense of the poor.

For this and many other things, Babylon must be destroyed now. Let me digress for a minute and talk to you about things that are happening that we have no clue about until the explosion happens. Now just recently, I came across an article that mentioned the N E R C. And it stands for Northern electrical resource corporation or something to that effect, it oversees the electronic power grid of America and they put out a report criticizing America's environmental social governance policies, basically saying we need to turn to green energy. Well, the report I read said that the supply of energy for the West and especially the Midwest will not meet the demand of this summer. Meaning we are headed for blackouts, no power for periods of time.

Now, if you have ever been in the south east, or live in a state with high humidity, you know how much of a danger it is to be without power. We are witnessing the Heavenly Father moving on a macro and micro level in ways we do not see but are being set in motion that will explode upon the earth with no remedy and nothing we can do about it. The NERC warning us that we do not have the resources to meet the demand coming on America in the west and especially the Midwest for this year because of dwindling resources and minerals and the closure of the electronic power plants in the Midwest.

For one reason or another. I want to speak more on these things but I've run out of time I will pick it up Heavenly Father willing in my next radio program. So, I want to give thanks to my Heavenly Father earthly mother for this incredible opportunity to be a light while I have been this reality.

And so, I'll see you again

Wednesday and Friday Pacific Standard Time.

Peace being to you

Shalom.

Only a week after the mass shooting in Buffalo comes news of another mass shooting in Texas. And to make matters worse this type of news no longer carries any real shock value. The politicians love to use these types of events for their own political gain, using events like this to draw on the sympathies and emotions of the people, to push agendas that will solidify loss of liberty and freedom in the name of safety. I heard a news commentator say today that America is suffering from a mental crisis. I certainly agree. When I received news of the shooting at the elementary school in which 18 children died, I immediately thought it may have been a revenge killing for what took place in Buffalo. The media did not say what the nationality was of the children and two adults was that died in the attack. All I can say is God help this nation if the news comes out that the children were white. It seems every day I find myself thinking I am actually witnessing the downfall of an empire the global empire of the oppressors of the Hebrew Israelite 12 tribes of Israel. It is starting to build in Europe with the threats being handed out by the Russian President and more recently the Belarusian president of certain nuclear war. It seems to me this is the way the God of Abraham Isaac and Jacob speaks to his children telling them to prepare to meet him and to give an account of ourselves to him. This is a nation and reality that without a shadow of a doubt has lost any fear of the God of Abraham Isaac and Jacob and the judgment to come. Also, it seems to me that America is Being exposed economically. It seems to me that America sees the other nations using their own currency to trade in and backing their currency with gold while excluding the American dollar which will force this nation to find other revenue streams and war is a great money-making machine. We have passed the point of no return and the feeling I get from watching the world through my TV screen is a subdued acceptance of the reality of impending nuclear war.

May God help us

Trumpets and red flags

Brethren it the times are very perilous, I have a website where you can join me for fellowship with other like-minded brethren and sisters, twelvetribesisraelites.com if anything I say resonates with you. You can get in contact with me. I have a room on Facebook where you can come and have fellowship with myself and other sons and daughters of light for the purpose of storing up and redeeming the time while it is day. Now I like to write books and you can go to Amazon and type in my name yaiquab yisrael. If you want to purchase a book that I have written where basically, I write diaries about the reality that I see and I try to do it from a biblical spiritual Hebrew Israelite perspective. So go to Amazon type in my name, and you should see the selection of books that I have written.

Okay, tonight, I wanted to name the title of the program, "trumpets and red flags". And the reason should be obvious why I would choose a title like that. Ever since I can remember. I have never seen a period of time that we have been seeing for the past three years ever since the timeline of the 400 years, came to its conclusion. Now, let me say a word about the recent mass shooting in Texas and Buffalo and allow me to speak a word about the difference between this kingdom and the kingdom of the God of Abraham, Isaac, and Jacob the biggest difference is that events such as the recent mass shootings will be a thing never, ever heard of. The big picture of the Israelite gospel is the restoration of the sons of light to eternal rulership. After the current beast Kingdom has run its course. Part of that restoration that you sons of light will have is the ability to know the thoughts that arise in men's hearts to strike evil against their fellow man. Sons of light will be able to defeat the evil thought before it bears fruit so in other words, even before those two men who committed the mass shooting would have been struck down even before they could pick up a rifle and go about doing the evil that is in their heart because a son of light will be able to know what is in their heart and strike them before they seek to accomplish their evil deed.

That is what came to my mind when I thought about the shooting in Texas and how our kingdom will be different. We will not need plans and other actions to defeat those who have evil in their heart. We will not need to try to come up with ways to stop events like this. You sons of light will be able to know what is in the oppressors heart and strike them. Just like the apostle did. Remember, in the book of Acts, when the two people try to withhold part of the money and they were struck down because I Peter asked, why have you allowed this thought to arise in your heart and He struck both of them down because he knew what was in their heart, and the same will be for you sons of light. I Want to say something that crossed my mind right before I came on the radio and I'm sure many of you have probably thought the same thing over and over again. About if men fear the God of Abraham, Isaac and Jacob like they should, we would not be hearing of not only these mass shootings that we have been seeing we would not see any evil. What so ever. People forget the wrath of God. People forget the fear of God. People forget there is such a thing called judgment. And we are already witnessing the first rain drops of judgment on our oppressor nations because they have forgotten the God of Abraham, Isaac, and Jacob. Brethren let me say something about an article that I came across a few nights ago. Do you know that there are three to six months of global wheat supply left according to the Guardian newspaper? And according to the I M F. The BIS bank an international bank that deals with settlements. Even the Bank of America stated there are only a few more weeks of food supply left. I also saw an article where India last year exported 37 tons of wheat. Do you know how many tons they have exported this year? Zero. They have nationalized their wheat crop meaning they do not have enough to export and trade with the world. And I also saw articles stating the same thing about different countries. One of them in particular halting its trade and exporting of sunflower oil and other forms of cooking oil because they do not have enough to trade, with other countries. They foresee revelation six and the prophecy about wheat and barley and how it will become too expensive for the majority of the world.

The scripture says it will cost a day's wage for a quart of wheat this is how the Heavenly Father blows his trumpets. This is how the Heavenly Father warns you Hebrew Israelite sons and daughters of light of impending judgment. And this is how the Heavenly Father is telling you to get your house in order. In John 14 We read where Judas not Iscariot ask Messiah "How will out manifest thyself unto us and not unto the world". And Messiah responded and said, "If a man loves Me, he will keep my word. And me and the Father will come and make Our abode we with him". Now, does anyone see how red flags and trumpets can be blown? All over the world? Yet you will not hear the oppressor, nations fall down on their face and beg the God of Abraham, Isaac and Jacob for some way out of the judgment that has now come to this man's Kingdom.

 I stated a few videos back about the account of how Nebuchadnezzar was granted 15 more years. I stated that in the year 2008. The current kingdom should have very well been dissolved with the 2008 financial crisis. I stated that Is it a coincidence? that just like Nebuchadnezzar was granted 15 years from 2008 to 2022 is 15 years? and we are now seeing the unmistakable confluence of events showing those who are looking for Messiah that most definitely the seals of Revelation are now being opened Brethren, I want to say something that I have been reminding us about for the past few weeks. I don't think that 2022 means the end of the extension, I believe that has been given to America but most certainly it is close. I do believe that since 2008. America has been given a reprieve that has run out. I have been speaking of probably the most powerful sign that I have ever seen which is the reappearance of Pluto and the 249-year cycle that ends in 2024. Brethren this is what you call a red flag and a trumpet that is speaking to our nation that if you are going to redeem the time and store up for yourself now is that time. I have a room on Facebook. I am a fisher of men. My only desire is to help you hopefully to want to do ministry or to help you to maintain fruitful faithfulness in your walk. This is a day and age where the strange woman of Proverbs five is taking the world away from the fear and knowledge of the God of Abraham, Isaac and Jacob now I want to mention something else that I saw in a recent video that I thought was amazing. It just so happens that right around the end of the month, the 28th and on, there will be a conjunction of Jupiter and Mars and it will form a red horn in the sky like the horn of Satan. Now I also read where the World Economic Forum chose this time to have one of their meetings to discuss further how they will implement different agendas that will help them in implementing their program of depopulation and other agendas that will enslave his fellow man. Now that lets you know that the oppressor nations, they watch the skies as well. They know that is where the truth and warning the God of Abraham, Isaac and Jacob reveals his timetable.

The Elite watch what goes on in the heavenlies I'm sure you probably already know. So, we should remember now is a time where any day now, any day now you sons and daughters of light may suddenly leave this reality. Now I say that because when you look at the "X" across America and consider that means it is finished. And then when you consider things that must come to pass before then. And then when you consider First Thessalonians chapter five, and how we are not appointed to wrath. You should be able to conclude in your mind that one 2024 Is the end meaning anything and everything that is going to be accomplished will be accomplished before then. Now, I could be wrong. But that is what I perceive as of right now. I also seem to believe that nuclear war is the end because of the inability to be able to survive it. And anyone that is looking for Messiah should clearly be able to see the brink of nuclear war that we are currently experiencing.

Anyone listening to the different prognosticators on the internet warning the children of Israel, should clearly be able to see that a nuclear war is imminent. That means you sons and daughters of light must leave before then. Before that happens. Allow me to digress for a second and speak on something else that I came across about how Israel and the United States are planning to have war games right around the end of May 2022. simulating an attack on you guessed it, Iran. Iran now, the seriousness of a war game is it could be a cover for an actual attack. They plan this right at the end of the month around the last week of May 22. Again, is it any coincidence that these things are happening right at around the time of the Mars Jupiter conjunction? that when you look at it in the sky, it forms a red horn. I find that quite amazing.

Brethren Did you know that recently Iran suffered a 300% increase in flower-based food supplies 300% increase in flower-based food supplies. And there was recently riots because of that in Iran. Brethren, that is what is coming to America. The war in the Ukraine has greatly diminished the supply of fertilizer of herbicides of barley of wheat of sunflower oil, and we are basically existing on what's in the pipeline right now before we begin to see the effects of the food shortage of Revelation chapter six. Take hold of this nation. Allow me to share a quick story about how I see inflation taking hold with my own eyes. Recently, my neighbors have been borrowing money and I find it to be no coincidence because of the rising gas prices. The rise in food prices that they are all of a sudden needing to borrow money. I can only imagine what families with children are suffering right now. It is a small indicator to me that the judgment of revelation six is creeping upon this nation in a way that we will not be able to deal with. Did you Brethren hear that just recently Hungary just declared a war time state of emergency over the war in Ukraine. Meaning they are preparing for imminent nuclear hostilities Did anyone hear what the Belarusian president said? In warning the western countries supplying weapons to Ukraine that it could lead to World War Three brethren.

I am a fisher of men. I am begging anyone under the sound of my voice to join me on Facebook. And let me minister to you so that you might bear fruit while we have time in this reality. The red flags and trumpets are louder and louder and this is the way the God of Abraham, Isaac and Jacob speaks to you. This is how the God of Abraham, Isaac and Jacob appears to you and not to the world. If you love his word, as it says in John 14, they are abiding with you and letting you know the time you are in so that you may prepare to appear before the God of Abraham, Isaac and Jacob. With something to offer, which is your life.

I want to give thanks to my heavenly father or mother for this incredible opportunity. Join me Wednesday and Friday 8pm Pacific Standard Time. And until I see you again, make peace be unto you to

Shalom

Playin us

Watching the NBA championship game today and immediately it made me mad, why is it that every time there is a big sporting event where it is primarily Hebrew Israelite Negros dominating the sport, they always seem to start it off with a Israelite woman singing praises to this country by way of the national anthem. It really burns my behind to see this form of Stockholm syndrome that still exists in our Nation Today. It shows me how much people love Vainglory as well. The oppressor nations in particular America seemed to think that if they can get Hebrew Israelite men and women to sing to the God of Abraham Isaac and Jacob in their favor that it will make everything go well with them and their nation. I get so mad when I see how the oppressor nations use us like they do and also seeing how those of our nation are willing to play to the desires of those who hate us. I wish I could get over things like our nation singing praises to our presentation by singing their national anthem but it just bugs me to no end. Tell me how come if we are such a Christian nation, we do not start out all sporting events with the recital of Psalm 23 or some other Bible verse or a prayer led by one of the children of Israel. The answer is because the evil that this country engages in and corruption is so great if we tried to begin all important events with acknowledging the God of Abraham Isaac and Jacob the heavenly father would probably send a lightning bolt that very minute someone would begin to open their mouth to begin the prayer or acknowledgement of the God of Abraham Isaac and Jacob. Hypocrites

Venezuela is coming to America

Hello and thank you for joining me. My name is yaiquab ban yisrael, and this is the Israelite sons of light radio program. I want to give thanks to my Heavenly Father earthly mother for this incredible opportunity they have allowed me to have where I can take my life energy and use it to the best of my ability to be a light to the God of Abraham, Isaac and Jacob and for my nation, the Hebrew Israelites, the people of Negro, Latino and Native American descent on their father's side. This is a radio program that is strictly for the purpose of fishing for men and women who resonate with the things that I say that have to do with the will of the God of Abraham, Isaac, and Jacob which is basically to be a testimony somehow, while you are in the daytime, which is now meaning the time before the door is closed, and there is no more opportunity to be about the will of our Father who art in heaven. And as I said, it is simply being a light and trying to minister to your nation, one way or another, to give them the knowledge that you have about the gospel as best as you can, in hopes that someone will hear you and they will turn and try to draw near to the God of Abraham, Isaac and Jacob okay.

The title of the program tonight is Venezuela is coming to America. Venezuela is coming to America. And before I begin let me say this. I primarily am a fisher of men and women. You really don't have to listen to my radio program more than once or twice, or maybe three times to know what I am all about. I have a room on Facebook, where I invite you to let me minister unto you, in hopes that you will find it in your heart to minister to Israel in a way of your choosing. My only desire is to help you become a multiplying ministry to help you get started on the road to ministry or if not, my desire is simply to help you to stay focus on the kingdom to come and not the temporary beast kingdom that we are currently under.

Okay, as I was saying. The title of the radio program tonight is Venezuela is coming to America. I want to ask a question to anyone listening under the sound of my voice. If you do not know about the situation in Venezuela. Allow me to inform you that it is a country that is starving. If you go online and you type in anything having to do with

Venezuela, food riots. You will see what I mean. I saw a video earlier today and what I saw you would think it was a horror movie. Because of the amount the sheer multitude of people who have no food. Venezuela is truly starving. And it has been that way for a few years. Now, can you exist on one egg a day? I saw a video of a Venezuelan food blogger testifying that that is what many of her people are living on Venezuelan a daily basis. One egg a day or something equivalent to that. Brethren, I want you to understand when you look at what's going on in Venezuela you are looking at what's coming to America. You will see 1000s on top of 1000s of people lined up some showing up a day before to stand in line and pray that there is a food delivery to the local market so that they may be able to have something to eat for that day. Now, it was interesting to way I was led to look at the situation in Venezuela. I was able to minister to someone who contacted me from Venezuela. And after getting to become a little familiar with the person she stated the living situation in her country was nearly unbearable. And so, I had an opportunity to minister to her. And then a couple of days ago she contacted me requesting to be ministered to again and I told her I could not minister to her every single time she requested because in the process of having done ministry for these 10 or 11 or 12 years have been defrauded many a time by my own nation. And I declined her request for that reason. And wouldn't you know it a couple of hours later out of nowhere. A video came to my attention about you guessed it, Venezuela and the food situation there, immediately I got the message. And I contacted her to let her know. I have sent you something to minister unto you. To me that was the Heavenly Father speaking to me, telling me that the person was telling me the truth. Her situation is dire. Feel free to minister unto her. And so, I did.

Now, let me say this before I go on if anyone wants to join me in ministering to this sister contact me and let me give you her info whereby you may be able to minister to her through her PayPal account. If you want to see what is coming to America, again, let me say to you, go to the internet and type in anything that has to do with the food shortage. Just like it says in Revelation chapter six verse six, and you will see live and in living color what is coming to America. How come? We don't have $40 billion dollars for Venezuela. Like we had for the Ukraine. Could it be that the situation in Venezuela is because they are staunch supporters of Catholicism? Latin people are the staunchest supporters of Catholicism that I know of. Could it be a result of their worship of the white Messiah? Other South American countries do not seem to have these types of problems that Venezuela has, and then I thought again, America is famous for destabilizing countries that do not play ball with them. And anyone will tell you that Venezuela has one of the biggest supplies of crude oil which is unrefined oil in the world. And when the United States recently cut off all oil imports from Russia. They came running to Venezuela after years of economic terrorism against that country and sending economic hitmen to Venezuela. All of a sudden, America had to come back with hat in hand begging them for increased oil trade.

Now as I was saying before, from what I can see the food shortage crisis in Venezuela has been going on for a few years now. And I know relations between Venezuela and America have not always been great. And so, I perceive that another reason for the crisis going on right now is because they will not deal with America on a level that America desires meaning they will not ship or trade their oil at a price that America desires. I could be wrong, but I know that in an oil rich country like that there is no reason that everyone cannot have enough food to eat. It makes no sense what so ever unless as I was saying before, that they are undergoing a judgment for worshipping, idolizing a white Messiah. But then you would have to ask the question, well, how come other countries do not suffer the same fate as Venezuela? I do not have an answer. The Heavenly Father knoweth. But I do know that in the world today the earthly mother is certainly able to supply basic food needs for everyone on the face of the earth. A thought that came to my mind is there is such a thing as free energy. But the powers that be the gods of this world refuse to share that information. That is the mystery behind the pyramids and the ley lines. And electromagnetic scientific technology that the gods of this world will not share with mankind because there is no profit, so that the few of this world may live high and mighty, while the rest of the global population suffer. They will not share the knowledge of free energy so that people can farm their own land. They can trade their own products; they can become self-sufficient.

Part of the reason is because the knowledge of free energy is not being shared. I recently saw a video of a Nigerian man who found a way to tap into free energy. They showed a video where a flat screen TV was playing a program it was not plugged into anything and all it had was a self- sufficient power supply. In the back of the flat screen TV. I have seen videos of vehicles running on water. I've seen videos of vehicles that run for miles and miles and miles but this information is not allowed to come out because it would destroy the oil and gas industry and this reality is profit driven to the exclusion of maybe over 80% of the global population. Meaning the current world government system is a system where the powers that be want to be served want to have control, want to have dominion, want to replace the worship of the god of Abraham, Isaac and Jacob and give it to them self. We are in a situation right now. Where the time is come for the eternal kingdom of the Hebrew Israelites and the powers that be know it and they seem to think if we cannot have the earth, no one can have the earth and that explains the current agendas of depopulation. Because if they can't have it, you can't have it either. Remember the account in the demon possessed man of the Gatorades when he came and met Messiah and Messiah cast the demons out of the man. Do you remember what the demons said? They said, have you come to destroy us before the time? the demons know when their time is up. The gods this world they know when this time is up. That is why things are speeding up. The various vaccine programs, the never-ending variants. They want you to remain afraid they want to kill your immune system. They want to make you subject to 5G technology where you may be remotely killed and if you don't believe what I am talking about, again, go online and type in something to the effect of man is killed remotely with 5G signal sent from a tower or something to that effect. That is the level that technology is on. There are certain elite who are warning the world that since this technology has been brought online in mass this year. Speaking of 5g technology this fall, we will begin to see the devastation of the current 5g technology in its ability to mass depopulate the earth, now I don't want to sound like I am fear mongering. I have always said on my videos if I perceive trouble. I am like the family dog. I will start barking whether the trouble is real or imagined and I will not stop warning our nation. But let me digress if I may for a second. Also, this fall there is another event that signals the absolute impossibility that this government can continue. There are some of you who may not know there is a movie called 2000 Mules, which has been recently in the news. It shows irrefutably how the election was stolen. From Donald Trump. It shows you people putting bags of votes into ballot boxes. Now, the Democrats were the ones shown to primarily be behind this. Now I could give a damn about American politics. And the only reason I am bringing this up is because it is the Democratic Party that is refusing any investigations into the allegations of election fraud. But this is a year that we are now in the midterms where the house the Congress of the United States may switch parties and the Republicans may come into power and they will have the authority to investigate the Biden administration and their son Hunter for money laundering for election fraud. And this type of thing could very well cause a nationwide rebellion against the government. It could very well cause the American public to trigger a civil war because of the corruption of government. It is common knowledge of the corruption that many of the current leaders are engaged in with money laundering with kickbacks sending money $40 billion dollars only to have a portion of it come back to government officials.

That is why this fall when investigations are conducted. And the truth comes out. This along with other confluence of events, many of which I have not even talked about. But Heavenly Father willing I will in the near future. Brethren draw nearer to the God of Abraham, Isaac and Jacob. I have a room on Facebook. Let me help you to remain focused on spiritual things. We are a nation that has been destroyed by the powers that be so that it is hard for us to even react to words of faith.

I want to give thanks to my Heavenly Father or tween my wind for this incredible opportunity.

Join me Wednesday and Friday 8pm Pacific Standard Time and until I see you again. peace be unto you

Shalom.

May 27 entry

Right after I finished doing my Friday video, I came across another video with this title the Russian foreign minister has stated that **"the West has declared war on Russia"** *the foreign minister said this because the United States Congress is authorizing long-range missiles for Ukraine in the conflict with Russia. Brethren Brethren truly truly the United States is playing with fire and Russia certainly will not allow this type of Weaponry to go to the Ukraine without consequences, because these long-range missiles can strike Moscow does anyone understand the gravity of this situation?*

Do you Brethren truly understand the gravity of the situation??!! This just cannot be happening these news events just cannot be real

June 1ˢᵗ 2022

Diary diary man I gotta tell you my mind lately seems to be in Overdrive. The confluence of events in the world today really boggles my mind because you would think it would cause the majority of this world to fear the fact that the truth will come out and that those on the wrong side of history will pay a price for it. I find myself thinking about the powers that be and the corruption of men in this current reality, there seems to be no thought No Fear no concern at all that the truth will come out and every man's heart will be shown for what it truly is whether for good or for evil the truth will come out. I find that this is what drives me to the God of Abraham Isaac and Jacob the truth will come out the secrets of the hearts of men will come out, if we do not have any concern to repent of all evil the truth will come out and there will be a recompense either way by the God of Abraham Isaac and Jacob and I find this is the driving force of my life and probably is for all people such as myself. The fear and reality and the love of the God of Abraham Isaac and Jacob is very real to people like me, but not to the world I live in and that is something that daily vexes me because there is no rhyme or reason for people to live and unbelief.

It's gonna change

Today I was watching a documentary on the 1%, meaning the people of the world who are so rich that they are richer than the 99% of the people in the world. Documentaries like this would and still do but not to as great an extent as they used to, make me mad as hell. I know from the Bible this is a judgment against the Hebrew Israelites 12 tribes of Israel the Negro Latino and Native American on their father's side. And this type of judgment I know is meant to produce a feeling of anger and regret for the fact that the children of Israel are the ones to blame for this situation we are currently in. The magnitude of wealth that the 1% own is staggering. I used to be mad as hell at seeing documentaries like this but now I say more power to them. This is the blessing of the oppressor nations. But if they knew what I knew about the eternal Kingdom they would trade places with me and my people in a heartbeat, even though we are poor for the most part afflicted we are the tail and not the head the whole world knows of the injustices that we suffer especially at the hands of law enforcement and our history of slavery oppression, but yet and still if the world knew who we are they would trade places with us in a moment of time. All the trillionaires of the world would trade places with the Hebrew Israelites in a moment if they knew who we are and what our Kingdom is, when we are restored. The tragedy is that my nation the Hebrew Israelites have been overcome for the most part by the pull of the world on their senses. The desire for money their desire to cater to the things of the flesh and Vainglory have overrun my own nation. The elite of my nation will not stand up and risk their prosperity for the sake of truth. I find it interesting that now when I watch documentaries like the blessing of the wealthy and elite of this world, I turn it around and imagine this documentary is talking about what the future Kingdom of our nation will be and the privileges that come with the eternal Kingdom of the God of Abraham Isaac and Jacob. I find that when I think that way and turn it around when I see documentaries about the privileged instead of it being a curse on my soul it becomes a blessing.

Very interesting

The beast kingdom

Man, oh man in fact it just find a way to shut my mind off and the sights and sounds of my reality life would be truly sweet. I came across some insight on the sugar industry in Florida in which Israelites really are continuing on in modern day slavery. And this is all just fine with the government state local and federal. The workers are Negros. Now to make matters worse it many a time is our own kind oppressing our own nation. A case in point is the brothers who own a huge part of the sugar production industry in Florida. Cubans are the tribe of Manasseh, part of the 12 tribes of Israel. They worked their workers long hours an average of 10 workers a year die in the sugar industry they are underpaid and there is nothing they can do for justice. And those who profit off of the misery of these Israelites could care less. That is how I know or at least one of the reasons I know the nag Hammadi is speaking the truth in categorizing the current reality as the beast Kingdom. Be Hebrew Israelites are currently in captivity to the beast Kingdom. The drug that America is addicted to is free labor and money making. This place is the beast Kingdom absolutely devoid of any fear of the God of Abraham Isaac and Jacob. The sugar cane workers in Florida sure modern-day slavery the politicians know it they will do nothing about it. There is only one small caveat. The God of Abraham Isaac and Jacob will do something about it. The children of Israel will be recompensed and that is something I believe in my heart and makes me keep ministering and going in spite of the great opposition of the world to truth and justice and the law of the God of Abraham Isaac and Jacob.

No one is getting away with anything

And I say Halaljah

WORK FOR IT

Yes, it is. Hello, and thank you for joining me. My name is Yaiquab yisrael. And this is the Israelite sons of light radio program. I want to thank you for joining me. I want to give thanks to my Heavenly Father earthly mother for this incredibly immense opportunity to be a light while I am in this reality, which means to only be about my father, who art in heaven business, the God of Abraham, Isaac and Jacob. This is a radio program where I want to minister to my nation, the Hebrew Israelites, the Negro, Latino and Native American on their father's side, this is a program especially for you, in which I try to minister to you, to invite you to have fellowship with me and my other light brethren in my room on Facebook, where I want to help you to eventually evolve into ministry, or if not, then simply to encourage you on a daily basis to continue in the faith bearing fruit until the end of our captivity.

I write books on Amazon, you can type in my name, yaiquab yisrael and my books should come up. I have a website twelvetribesisraelites.com for ministry and information. I also have a room on Facebook, called the "upper room"

 now before I begin, allow me to digress for a moment I will bet any amount of money I say that facetiously that during the NBA championships that are starting tomorrow they will have a Hebrew woman singing the national anthem. Even after the buffalo shooting, the murder of George Floyd of Breonna Taylor of the 1000s of Hebrew Israelites who have been killed by the justice system of this nation. How much do you want to bet? There will be a Hebrew woman who they will trot out there to sing the national anthem. For that matter, how much do you want to bet that during the NBA championships, which has a global platform? How much do you want to bet that not a single Hebrew Israelite will take the opportunity to rock the boat and let the world know who the children of Israel are? There will not be a single brother I am sure that will take the opportunity to make a statement that would set the world on its behind. Just one statement, which would advance our cause, for who knows how long, it was just a little thought I had that our own nation, the elite among us will not jeopardize their own personal situation for the sake of filthy lucre or power and it is truly, truly a shame.

Now I entitled the name of the program tonight. "Work for it". Work for it. What I mean by work for it is a principle that we should be able to see in the Bible clearly. The kingdom of the God of Abraham, Isaac and Jacob is open to the Hebrew Israelites. Sons and Daughters of light. Now, I believe our nation will be the future blessed children of Israel in the eternal kingdom. But I do believe as I read that you sons and daughters are future kings and queens of the eternal kingdom. And we have been truly gifted to do what we do, to minister to our nation, even though we serve a nation, meaning our people, at least from my purview, who are very unthankful people, very unable to respond even on a less than semi regular routine. When the word goes out, we as sons and daughters of light, have been equipped to minister in spite of tremendous opposition and apathy.

A principle that is clear in the world is if you desire to live the life you want to live, then you must work for it. If you intend to live on the highest level of society. You must separate yourself by way of study, research, discipline, ability and you must be able to endure your reality. That is a common principle in the world today that few people are able to accomplish. They know that in order for them to live the reality they truly desire you must work for it and it is the same way for the kingdom of God. You sons and daughters of light must work for it.

In this reality, you must go to work. You must do it consistently. You do it for compensation. Even when you do not want to go to work. You know you better go to work. If you know what is good for you. Now, the principle in the world is the same in the kingdom of the God of Abraham, Isaac and Jacob. There are some of you in our nation who have been given the ability to minister no matter come hell or high water. You find it within your soul. That you will minister which means you will be a light of the God of Abraham, Isaac and Jacob no matter what the situation because you cannot help yourself and I know the same is true for me.

When you desire to draw nearer to the God of Abraham, Isaac and Jacob and you are sincere and you endure the testing the Holy Spirit and the things she will put you through. If you can endure you will reap a harvest. The same principle in the world is true and the kingdom of the God of Abraham, Isaac and Jacob. The difference is that the God of Abraham, Isaac and Jacob gives you the Holy Spirit to endure mentally, physically. Even while we are in the midst of the Beast kingdom, surrounded by the oppressor nations, you Hebrew Israelite sons and daughters of light find that you are able to concentrate and meditate on the things of God. His Word on his son Messiah. You find that you are able to cater your actions in line with the desire spiritually to serve the God of Abraham, Isaac, and Jacob. We must work for it, anything worth having requires a sacrifice. I read in the fourth book of Enoch. And I'm sure many of you have read the same thing. It is a very serious verse where we are told that at first, the entrances to the kingdom of God was wide and broad and then when we fell the entrances to the kingdom of God became straight and narrow. As it says in Matthew chapter seven, the kingdom of God is described as a city set on a hill. The question is posed in the fourth book of Enoch How shall we gain our inheritance if we do not at first overcome the path laid out of affliction, oppression and vexation the Heavenly Father has put before us?

 the blessing of the kingdom of God means affliction, it means overcoming. It means endurance daily because of the high calling of the God of Abraham, Isaac and Jacob. The kingdom of God requires sons and daughters to endure and be consistent and aspire to minister to our nation.

Now I want to digress for a moment and speak on the incredible overcoming that your sons and daughters must do to obtain the city on the hill. I recently read and saw a video on the Rwandan massacre. Some of you may have heard about the genocide of the Tutsi people of Rwanda in 1994. You may recall there was a civil war. I saw an incredible video where it is coming out that a doctor named Pierre Gilbert, a French doctor makes an astounding incredible claim that the Rwandan genocide were 200,000 to 500,000 people were killed. Get this… may very well have been the result of a magnetic vaccine experiment that was able to be inflicted upon the Hutus through a vaccination program that caused them to basically become walking talking breathing zombies able to commit such atrocities.

Now anyone listening to the sound of my voice, this doctor, Dr. Pierre Gilbert, who you can find on bitchute a platform similar to YouTube. If you type in his name, you may be able to come across his video that he gave in the 1990s warning the world that science was approaching a level of being able to control people's actions through electronic frequencies. He tried to give this information to his government who immediately shut him down and forbid him from continuing on with that research. There was another doctor in this country. A doctor Bise B I S E. You can look him up, who gave the same warning that stated that in the near future artificial intelligence and science, we're going to be able to manipulate human beings through electromagnetic scientific technology. And he was forbidden further research on the subject by our own government who realize the ramifications if word got out the rebellion of the people would be uncontrollable against the government. The government knew full well they weren't going to have their own scientists develop this program. You guessed it, to control you and to implement their depopulation. program like they did in Rwanda in my humble opinion, that was an experiment. It worked marvelously. As usual. They conduct these things First, on the brown people of the planet.

They saw that it worked. They developed it and now here we are in 2022 where technology has gotten to a point where the vaccinations have a substance in them called graphene oxide which makes you subject to 5G soon to be six g and do you know that the warning is now going out? If you type in doctors like Dr. Professor, Dolores Cahill. Bitchute Dr. Shirley Tenpenny Dr. Peter Yeadon a former head of Pfizer warning the implications of the current vaccination program and the agenda behind it. Dr. Robert Malone. Doctor Dr. Kerry Ardis among 1000s of doctors warning you that the vaccinations are a Trojan horse making its way into your temple, your body for the purpose of being able to control your thoughts, your emotions and your actions.

This is truly the beast kingdom. And you sons and daughters of life are threatened with this type of agenda. The population primarily against the Hebrew Israelite 12 tribes, we are witnessing Revelation chapter six, verse three. Right in front of our face if you desire, you can find information pointing to the food shortages that will increase especially later this year around August when you come across information about the crop harvest projections around the world and how dire they are. Then you will know what I am talking about. So, I want to say to you sons and daughters of light. We are on the verge of witnessing a nation and world of people soon to go Stark Raving crazy. Because when they knew God, they honored him not if God and now the door is shut and you sons and daughters of light are going to see a world of people and what happens when you do not have the mind to work and build your foundation and build a case of testimony. While the opportunity is there.

We do not want to work for what we cannot see. Because spiritually we have been taught to be lazy, but I want to say to you sons and daughters of light. We are being surrounded by incredible info the same thing that happened to the people of the Rwandan genocide who most likely were part of an experiment. The same thing in my humble opinion is going to happen again on a global scale and the level of blood flowing to the horse's bridle will be unlike anything we could ever imagine.

You brethren who are laboring This message is for you. I know that it is very difficult sometimes to want to continue and endure because of the apathy that we see around us and the two thirds of our nation. But I want to say to you, the confluence of events really should make us rejoice. We are coming to the end of our captivity and sentence and all that is left is the kingdom of God. And the downfall of the oppressor nations.

So please, if anyone under the sound of my voice can hear me, I am a fisher of men. I offer an opportunity to be in our midst so that I may use my gift to invite you to have fellowship with this where I minister to you on a daily basis. Try to help you focus on the spiritual and not the physical or the current reality. I try to help you endure to the end of our captivity join me my room called the upper room on Facebook send me a friend invite for one to give thanks to my Heavenly Father earthly mother for this incredible opportunity. Join me Wednesday and Friday 8pm Pacific Standard Time and until I see you again. peace be unto you

shalom,

THE TRUTH

it is really true?
but still, I refuse to believe
How the truth
Cannot be received

I'm talking to you America
Every day
You never fail
To amaze me

The spell you cast
On the people of all types
Teachers educators
PHD's high and mighty

Doesn't matter
No ability
To discern what is right
Lies prosper

All you need
Is enough corruption
Spread all around
Mainly from men wearing ties

To deceive the people
To call the truth a lie
Right to the face of
To the God of Abraham Isaac

And Jacob

Actually believing
Your own evil agendas
To depopulate
The whole civilization

And to starve others

Into submission
And others
Mindless robots

Through endless vaccinations
No way can you be serious

Actually believing
Really really believing
That you will get away with it

You're mistaken

The most high never sleeps
The angels never cease
Documents and testimonies
On the increase

To serve as a witness
Of the violence against
The truth tellers
Who shined the light

on the flow of blood
From the Hebrew Israelites

An evil and wicked
Generation
Who would not
Who could not

Fear what is eternal
The righteous Kingdom
Be afraid America
The truth cannot be defeated

Although presently
Very few can speak it
Even less to agree with it
But the truth will win

The truth about
Who really started it
The evil corruption
The lust and money loving

And greed and murder
And self-seeking secret agendas
Only for a moment
Can they escape judgment

How come the elite?
How come the educated?
Cannot see or understand
The honest truth when it is spoken?

Like when the Bible says
I am sending you a famine
Like when the Bible says
I will judge all evil ways

Like when the Bible says
Messiah will come again?

What has the truth done
To deserve
The love of darkness
Of sin and iniquity?

How is it we have arrived
At this point in life
Where we cannot tell evil
Even when right before our eyes?

How much longer
Before

Too late too late
Will arrive

I'm afraid it may already
Be here

I testify

Hello, thank you for joining me. My name is yaiquab ban yisrael. And this is the Israelite sons of flight radio program that I like to try to do every Wednesday and Friday. Today is a Saturday and I usually do my shows Wednesday or Friday 8pm Pacific Standard Time. Before I begin, I want to give thanks to my Heavenly Father earthly mother for this incredible opportunity that I have, which is to be a light shining the way to the God of Abraham. Isaac and Jacob. Like my other Israelite brethren, a chance to minister and to show my Father who art in heaven, what I would do if he gave me that opportunity to build a testimony to glorify the God of Abraham, Isaac and Jacob and I couldn't be more thrilled even though I'm afflicted I'm disabled all sorts of vexations and oppressions. But I could not be happier.

Now I am a fisher of men. I find a desire to do exactly as Messiah did to seek and search for that which was lost the Hebrew Israelites Negros, Latinos and Native Americans on your father's side. That is what my ministry is about. I have a room on Facebook called the upper room. There I am wearing the green and white garment. My desire is to have you come in, have fellowship with me and my other brethren and sisters, where I will post verses and do my level best to help you to focus and to figure out a way for you to hopefully evolve to do ministry, or to help you to bear the fruit of faith while we are in this reality. Now I also write books you can type in my name yaiquab yisrael on Amazon and my books. should come up.

But again, thank you for joining me there's a lot going on in the world. And it should be very easy if you are spiritually minded. You want to be about the will of our Father who art in heaven. You should be able to see the contradiction of the world against what you know to be true, which is the eternal kingdom, the kingdom of the God of Abraham, Isaac and Jacob and is a kingdom of the Hebrew Israelite 12 tribes. If you are paying attention then you should be able to increase in faith as you look and you see a world of darkness surrounding you and getting greater. Now I entitled the name of the program tonight. "I testify" and from time to time, I just feel I want to testify of the things that have happened to me in my life. Personally, any brother ministering who cannot testify of the grace of the God of Abraham, Isaac and Jacob in his life. Is a brother that does not overstand the God of Abraham, Isaac and Jacob correctly. If you are going to be serious, and approaching the God of Abraham, Isaac and Jacob, if you are going to be sincere in ministry, for the God of Abraham, Isaac and Jacob, if you endure the trials and tribulations, that the Holy Spirit will put you through, you will come to a point where you will cut through falsehoods like a hot knife through butter.

Now I do not mean you will know everything about everything. But you will certainly learn the things that will help you to endure as you draw nearer to the God of Abraham, Isaac and Jacob. You will learn the things that will help you build a solid foundation. You don't have to worry about anything other than being sincere. Being consistent able to endure and the Holy Spirit will take care of the rest and build your foundation so that as you see the hope of the oppressor nations, of the Gentiles, of the people who say they are Jews and are not, slowly Brick by Brick falling down while your foundation gets stronger.

Currently, I am under suspension on you too. Which to me, is a badge of honor. I am under suspension for a week for telling the truth as best I can. The truth is not welcome. In this current reality, especially the Hebrew Israelite truth is not welcomed in this current reality even in the midst of our own nation. Many times, the truth is not accepted amongst even the 12 tribes of Israel. We don't like to be called out, we do not like to be challenged, to be dedicated, to point out sin and iniquity in our nation. Many times, we want to hear smooth things and not the stricter things of the faith. We do not many times seem to overstand that the road is narrow the Scriptures say and the way is as if there was deep water on one side and fire on the other on the way to the city on the hill. And I testify that our nation has fallen prey to easy believelism. We have fallen prey to Christianity and Catholicism where even now, many of us are unable to respond to the word of the heavenly father when it goes out.

I want to use an analogy as I am want to do from time to time. If you are in a relationship and I am approaching, it primarily from a male standpoint is if you are in a relationship and you arrive at a point where you are unable to respond to your wife because you don't care anymore. Or the feeling has died down. The thrill is gone. You will soon find yourself single in a relationship. You must respond to your spouse, or it cannot work. Right now. The word is Messiah. He was the Word made flesh. He is now back to being the word, but he draws no reaction from his own children many a times, it is a great source of vexation to me as one who loves to minister the word of Messiah and who loves and over stands. Messiah is the word if you do not... cannot... respond to Messiah. Then the coming days will prove a great vexation to you.

I have a room on Facebook where I am inviting you, the listener to come and join me and my brethren where I will try to minister to you where I try to beg you to store up for yourself and bear fruit yourself by taking advantage of the opportunity to minister to your brethren as the scripture says, Your works will follow you but we do not seem to realize that if we knew in our soul, every single verse we share with other brethren would pay us a billion dollars a letter, the room that I have on Facebook and other rooms similar to mine, Hebrew Israelite chat rooms would be overflowing. And brethren, I am here to say that is the case. When we draw nearer to the God of Abraham, Isaac, and Jacob, He will draw near to you. Now, I want to testify of something that happened to me two days ago and if I testify, I could go until Messiah comes back. I can talk like a girl when it comes time for me to testify of things and blessings. Good and bad. that have happened to me as I have been on this path of learning, the God of Abraham, Isaac, and Jacob and the things that come with it. Now I want to testify of something. As I was saying, that happened to me only a couple of days ago.
"

Now I shared on the video called Venezuela is coming to America". It's the last video on my YouTube channel. Before I was suspended. On that video, I shared an account of a Venezuelan sister who cried out for help and I shared how I was able to minister to her. But when she contacted me again my heart was hardened. And I ignored her request. And what after I ignored her request, I saw a video detailing and documenting the incredible food shortage situation going on in Venezuela, immediately I decided to minister to the sister immediately and I rebuked myself for my own hard heart which I find happens to me a lot. I have a history of mis judging people of falsely accusing people of not ministering when I should to people when it was in my ability. And this is part of the pain of drawing near to the Heavenly Father as he shows you your blessings and your curses and shows you your real self and things that you must get rid of as you learn to put on the garment of love and compassion.

So anyway, when I saw the video of what is going on in Venezuela, I looked at it as confirmation that my father who are in heaven was sending me a rebuke and I repented and I was able to minister to this sister in Venezuela, which I plan to continue doing. I also had a chance just last week to minister to the blessing of someone else. Now, the next day, for some reason. The spirit was on me to look for a certain vehicle that I wanted to purchase. Because being disabled, I need to use my legs more efficiently. Currently, I had a truck that I had to clutch in and shift and drive and brake at the same time many times. My legs do not move as fast as I tell them. So, driving my current vehicle is somewhat hazardous. Well, a couple of days ago after I was able to minister to the sisters, after which I' thought nothing about it. When the Spirit moved me to look at a vehicle that I wanted, do you know a couple of hours later I was sitting in that vehicle after having been given the opportunity and after having been rebuked for my heart heartedness. I was blessed with the vehicle I had been looking for. That would make it easier for me to drive. And it was interesting because my reaction is not what you may have thought it should have been. Now don't get me wrong I lit incense as a thanksgiving offering. I was full of praise I still am and I wanted to tell the whole world, but still I was resigned because I know we have come to the end of the world and the concluding events are fast approaching on the political front, the social front, the geopolitical front, the military front, the geopolitical front, the economic front. All these things are strangling the current reality. And I can see these things closing in clearly. And I'm not ashamed to say we have come to the end of this reality. And that is why my reaction to receiving my 2016 minivan was subdued in my opinion. Because there is a bigger picture. There is the day of the Lord. There is great tribulation, and it is right at our doorstep. The life that we always knew is coming to a conclusion and the only thing that will matter is that you have a testimony that you have built up that you can point to… to prepare for that day when we will be required to give an answer for what we did with our reality. I am speaking to you Hebrew Israelites. We are fast approaching the end of this reality, the end of power captivity, the end of the rulership of the oppressor nations, the end of Esau's blessing the end of the tribe of Japheth Reign of Terror, the so-called Jews, the fake Jews. We are looking at the end of this nightmare called America. We are witnessing Nahum chapter three right before your very eyes. Whoa to the bloody city. That's America. It is all full of lies and robbery.

The prey departeth not the noise of a whip and the noise of the rattling of the wheels and the prancing horses and of the jumping chariots, (meaning the military armies of America and the other oppressor nations). The horsemen lifted up the bright sword and the glittering spear and there is a multitude of slain and a great number of carcasses, and there is none end of their corpses. They stumble upon their corpses because of the multitude of the whoredoms of the well-favored harlot, the mistress of witchcrafts that sell the nations through her whoredoms and families through her which crafts. Behold, I am against thee, saith the LORD of hosts, and I will discover by skirts upon thy face and I will shew the nation's thy nakedness, and the Kingdoms by Shame and I will cast abominable filth upon thee, and make the file and we'll set the as a gazing stock and it shall come to pass that all day that look upon thee shall flee from thee and say Nineveh is laid waste, that's America, who will bemoan thee? When shall I seek comforters for thee? and brethren That is where we are right today.

The Heavenly Father has lifted the skirts of America who is Nineveh Who is the bloody city Who is the harlot, and her nakedness is being shown her corruption. There is nothing she can do except censor the truth and to silence the voice of the truth tellers because, her time has come. Russia is ready to strike America and silence her forever. All one has to do is pay attention to their many threats the more we send military lethal aid to the Ukraine and the responses and warnings that Russia is issuing. should let anyone know this is the God of Abraham, Isaac and Jacobs final call. You will not hear our voice much longer. The bride and the bridegroom say come to you Hebrew Israelites. While it is daytime we say come. I have a room on Facebook. Called the Upper Room. Send me a friend invite let me speak to you to see if it is the right fit for you. And to find out whether you may be a lively stone, meaning someone who can respond and share and participate 99% of people who come into that room at some point, stop sharing verses and stop offering their opinions and stop sharing things that might bless other brethren. Many brethren, at some point stop responding and that is a warning to consider before you consider joining me in my room. I want to give thanks to my Heavenly Father earthly mother for this incredible opportunity.

 Join me Wednesday and Friday 8pm And until I see you again.
peace be unto you,

Shalom

DESCENT

Once again, I have to move my pen in a writing direction that I really don't want to. This book is a diary and I want it to tell the truth the best as I know it and I want it to testify when the time comes of what I saw while I was in my reality. I am pretty sure that the God of Abraham Isaac and Jacob is showing me the conclusion of the experiment called planet earth. It seems that I am staring at inevitable World War three as I write this. Amazingly it seems like the past few years since we have heard about nuclear warfare so much it no longer has any shock value even when they speak of it on the mainstream media. It seems like America has a fascination with what nuclear war would be like. We seem to think that this is all a horror movie and that we will simply be able to say reset after we see what happens after a nuclear exchange between superpowers. It seems that America is bent on provoking Russia into a global confrontation and there is nothing anyone can do about it. The only thing that can prevent our descent into shore World War is the God of Abraham Isaac and Jacob, but I am afraid this is all going according to plan for the eventual restoration of the Hebrew Israelites currently in captivity to those who have historically oppressed us. It seems to me that the heavenly father wants men to see what happens when they believe that they can govern themselves better than he can.

We are living currently in June 2022 under a state of complete madness. It seems as if we have gotten tired of moving in relative peace and safety as a nation world true Mad Men have begun to scheme and imagine things in their mind about how they can carve up the world for their own benefit and to get rid of all the useless eaters such as myself being disabled along with old age people and maybe even people bent on committing crime or maybe even people with drug problems and other psychological maladies. It seems as if the powers that be want to live in a world where no one is imperfect only them and to make sure that they can live forever. To make a long story short with each passing generation with each passing month with each passing day man is showing why he must be destroyed he seems unable to prevent himself from trying to replace the God of Abraham Isaac and Jacob. The more his technology and science evolves the more it turns to pure insanity. The current events in the Ukraine or a long trumpet sounding for anyone who can hear to get ready to meet the God of Abraham Isaac and Jacob we are quickly descending into final reality.

May God help my nation the Hebrew Israelites and myself

SOMEBODY

Somebody somebody
Better tell America fast
Better tell America
Stop poking the Russian bear

Just what is it?
Why must we
Provoke and persist
Even a fool knows

It's not wise
To keep poking a bear
In the eyes

But you America
You just won't stop
Just what is it with
This foolish desire?

To destroy yourself?

To destroy your friends
For money and wealth
For power and domination

The bear is crying
Don't do this thing
Provoke us no more
Or what you fear

Will Tarry no more

Somebody somebody
Better tell America
After this world
There is no more

Your only opportunity

To do what is right
To redeem yourself
To make a case

For you to continue
Under great glorious blessing
That was given to you
The bear is pleading

The thing is ready
The trigger is cocked
The seconds run down
No prayers are left

America America
Repent
Turn away
From the hidden agendas
From the evil deception

Of the powers that be
Lusting for your blood

Who took advantage
Of long loss youth
You once knew
Until

Your virginity
Stolen and corrupted
Now resting in the hands
Of those who hate your guts

Somebody somebody
Somebody better tell America

Getting what you deserve

And this is the Israelite sons of light radio program. And before I begin, I want to give thanks to my Heavenly Father earthly mother for this incredible opportunity to try and do my best to be a light for the nation of Israel, you Negroes Latinos and Native Americans on your father's side. I am a fisher of men for you to try to help you draw nearer to the God of Abraham, Isaac and Jacob. Before I begin, I want to say that I am also a writer, and I simply write what you might call diaries. You type in my name yaiquab yisrael on Amazon, my books should come up. I have a website called twelveribesisraelites.com lowercase lettering all spelled together, where you can go for ministry and information you can get in contact with me there. I have room on Facebook for brethren to come and have fellowship with one another. Also, where I try to minister to you by way of posting verses from Gnostic texts, and Bible and any other books that I perceive are anointed books you may never have heard from before, my room is called the upper room on Facebook send me a friend invite and let me try to talk to you to see if the room is a good for that fit for you. I'm looking for lively stone, Hebrew Israelites sons and daughters of light, who know how to respond to the word as it goes out to seek to encourage other brethren and to redeem the time and to store up treasure because there is such a thing as Redeeming the time, and storing up for yourself a treasure in heaven that faded, not the way. I titled the name of the program. This evening is "get getting what you deserve".

There is a positive connotation to that. And a negative connotation to that. In my reality, it has been a great vexation to me every day when I look around and I see my nation waste wasting your reality, wasting time not storing up treasure for yourself this is your opportunity to write your witness in the Earth to find a way to be a light to the God of Abraham, Isaac and Jacob, being about our Father's business, which had great recompense of reward. If you can examine yourself and take advantage of the spirit you have within you to share spiritual things that you are learning for the glory of the God of Abraham, and Isaac, and Jacob and he will help you He will grant you His Holy Spirit. She will lead you and guide you into all wisdom that you need in order to endure this reality.

But the pull of the world is very strong and very effective on our nation to distract us to love filthy lucre to seek after the carnal desires of the flesh or to seek after the material things of the world. The pull of the world meant to take you away from the God of Abraham, Isaac and Jacob. The Kolbrin Bible says that as you grow older and you witness the course of the world you should realize everything remains the same. There is no new thing under the sun, at some point you should begin to consider your mortality. You will get what you deserve. Either way, you lively stone sons and daughters of life will get more than you deserve. The scriptures say we are in a time of momentary and light affliction. Momentary, temporary, and light affliction which will set the stage for your eternal future in the eternal kingdom, like the Kolbrin Bible says there should come a time when we consider the things that are most important. In other words, we should depart from dead works to the best of our ability at some point in our life. I recall reading in the Republic of Plato men reasoning and one commented to the other" service to the Heavenly Father. Endurance and consistency will be the nurse of your old age. You will find comfort in the things that you have built up whether great or small". As you see the world and its foundation slowly deteriorate, while yours gets stronger and stronger as you are able to look back on the things that you'd have built up spiritually. As the days go on, you will realize that you are slowly building a mountain for the God of Abraham, Isaac and Jacob and he will not only give you what you deserve, but more than you can ever imagine. Consider Psalm 34 Seven and I hope I am quoting that correctly. Where it says that he will give you the Heavenly Father the desires of your heart. Saw Psalm 34 Seven. Now, recently, I testified have an incredible blessing of being given the opportunity to minister in a couple of ways and for some reason, a vehicle that I had been wanting to purchase came to mind. I had concluded I would not be able to receive the vehicle because of my financial situation. I was able to minister to a couple of sisters and to make a long story short after researching and looking at the vehicle I wanted a couple of hours later, I was sitting in the vehicle, the Spirit came upon me to look at the vehicle. And this was shortly maybe a day after I was able to do a little ministry and the Spirit came on me to look at the vehicle I wanted and simple is that a couple of hours later, I was sitting in the vehicle.

Now I testify that it was not my doing that this thing happened. It's a blessing that I believe anyone who is sincere, who is consistent who wants to glorify the God of Abraham, Isaac and Jacob. They should have a similar testimony as this testimony. I have just shared. I can share until the cows come home testifying of the grace I have received in my reality. But I also say that the Heavenly Father cannot be ministered to only for the sake of the dainties of this current reality, the Heavenly Father cannot be ministered to only for the purpose of receiving the goodly things of this reality. There must be a sincerity a desire a willingness to be about our father's business. These things we will need in order to endure the vicissitudes of life in order to endure the apathy of the world.

Anything less than sincerity and truth will not build a solid foundation to help you Hebrew Israelite sons and daughters of light to endure this reality all the way to the end. The heart of the God of Abraham, Isaac and Jacob is to love others as you love yourself, to let the love of God be shed abroad in your heart to minister to your nation. To your people in sincerity and truth and you will see your testimony grow and grow and grow. You will be unable to keep silent as you see your foundation getting stronger and seeing your wisdom precede you and as you see the Heavenly Father using you, to minister and to be a light.

You will realize you are getting more than you deserve. Speaking to you lively stone, Hebrew Israelite sons and daughters of light. I want to say again, I have a room on Facebook, where you can send me a friend request and let me share with you the nature of the room and what I am looking for and the type of brothers and sisters I want to be a part of the room now there is a negative side to getting what you deserve. And I am referring mainly to the oppressor nations, who, as we speak, are on the very brink of the end of their reality and gift of rulership of the world. And the very brink of going in to captivity to the Hebrew Israelites, 12 tribes, Negros, Latinos and Native Americans on your father's side. We are currently in a reality that each day that goes by brings us closer and closer to 2024 When an absolutely incredible event will take place. It will be the conclusion of the cycle of Pluto and it will also initiate in April of 2024 for the "x" across America. The first slant went from north west to South East and in 2017 the first slant was done. In 2024 the opposite solar eclipse will go from North East to South West in 2024, forming an "x" across America.

Now consider what happens before the "x" Scripture says for those of you who are lively stone, sons of light that you will not suffer the wrath to come. The scripture says that we are not appointed to wrath in First Thessalonians five, we should clearly be able to see that now. The oppressor nations are getting what they deserve. I want to say again, Revelation chapter six, verse three is very, very clear. It speaks of inflation. It speaks of a financial reset. It speaks of a black horse. It speaks of judgment. America primarily and those who have oppressed the Hebrew Israelites are getting what they deserve. The message to the 12 tribes of Israel is to come home immediately. There is a storm. It is brewing it is on the horizon and it is leaving behind a path of destruction that no one will be able to endure.

Did anyone see the video that was leaked out from the Chinese military? There was a high-level meeting and they were discussing the invasion of Taiwan. Do you know that video was leaked out a week ago? Maybe two weeks at the most. The video exposed China's plan to invade Taiwan as if imminently now, brothers and sisters it is very easy for people such as myself to see judgment is now everywhere around. We have the agenda of depopulation. We have the current hostilities in the Ukraine. We have the dire warnings about food shortages. In addition to the warning of Revelation chapter six. We are witnessing in this country. An explosion in gas prices. Brethren, we are seeing judgment that is not being exposed in the mainstream. Messiah said to those that look for him shall he appear unto salvation. I want to say again to you Hebrew Israelite sons and daughters of light. Now is the time to come home immediately. The Heavenly Father has shown us His power to make the nations expose their own wickedness even to the present the oppressor nations, especially America, continue to show the Hebrew Israelites singing their national anthem singing and dancing and entertaining them or protecting their politicians. Something I only recently begin to realize they make fools out of us. They patronize us. They get us to sing their songs. And we fall for it every time even at a time when we are on the very brink, the very brink of the end of this reality. We are a nation of people. The Hebrew Israelites. We are literally dying to forgive our enemies. We do not seem to realize that the Heavenly Father is a God of Recompense. We have reached a point in our reality where our oppressors mainly Americans, Christians, Catholics, Europeans, realize there is no turning back. The last thing they want to hear is the Hebrew Israelites speaking the truth about their judgment, the reality of the Eternal Kingdom the reality of Recompense that will be double what we endured. They will get what they deserve. The oppressor nations. If anyone has been listening lately, the threats from Russia are becoming more and more ominous. If anyone is paying attention, Russia seems to have resigned itself to the inevitability of nuclear war coming to this nation and world they seem to have come to grips with the fact that there will be a World War three, there will be nuclear war. That's what America wants. They realize that America is in desperate straits economically, because we cannot compete with the different nations trading amongst themselves, pegging their currency to gold. America realizes that the only way to endure is to instigate war, because war, as I have said before, is profit. Brethren, have you heard of the st Malachy Prophecy? The prophecy predicting that the current pope will be the last pope? Do you know that an article came out a couple of days ago that he is most likely ready to retire?

Now look at the st Malachi prophecy. It has a history of previous prophecies that were a pass list listing all the Pope's and listing who the last Pope would be. Second, the article said that this pope is ready to retire. And if the st Malachi prophecy has any credibility to it, which I believe it does, because of the confluence of events at this time. Then brethren, I would say to anyone listening to the sound of my voice. It is time to come home to the father immediately. Right now, that means to forsake the world to become a light sharing spiritual truths being about your father's business, the God of Abraham, Isaac, and Jacob right now. Brethren, I want to thank you for joining me Wednesday and Friday on blog talk radio to 8pm I try to have my programs but I have recently been banned from YouTube for a week. So, I will see you next week Heavenly Father willing on YouTube and until I see you again.

Peace be until you
Shalom

For a reason

Interesting thought I had today everything is here for a reason 60% of the things do not make sense to me like self-seeking in Vainglory and all forms of evil and hatred and godlessness. But all these things are here for a reason, it is probably best that we not know the reason for the good and the evil completely. It seems humanity would not be human if we were perfect. There is a reason four relationships of all kinds, the only thing I can conclude in my mind is to show us all forms of psychological mental makeup of the human experiment. There is a reason for all these things which is to show us that we need to be a theological society totally submitted to the God of Abraham Isaac and Jacob. In my life the common denominator of the lessons that I have learned is that we must be guided supernaturally there is no way to legislate or two can find the human heart 100% in a way where man can live in peace and harmony with one another forever other than to submit to the heavenly father the God of Abraham Isaac and Jacob. I know I'm saying nothing new but I want to write about it because the lesson is so recurring to me. I want to be able to look back at my mindset many years from now and remember the things that I struggled with and trying to understand all things pertaining to my reality. People will be people having their positives and negatives of spirit and soul. But I am absolutely amazed at the power of self-seeking godless Vainglory and idolatry of this current reality. I must resign myself to the fact that this is just the way things must be in order for the greater eternal Kingdom to come in all its fullness. Life is truly a lesson of opposites meaning it takes one to make the other greater either for the good or for the evil

June 9th 2022

Mad politics

The people came to visit
The nation's capital
And history was made
Not just because

It was my mom's birthday

No history was made
Because the politicians were afraid
Meaning mostly white people
Hiding in the capitol building

Because outside
People were rioting
The president incited the people
To take revenge

Because the election he did not win

Politicians are mostly Caucasian
And January 6
The people came to visit
Because the president wasn't too happy

And wanted revenge
Against the mostly Caucasian
Politicians
And they were mighty afraid

Because the crowd became a mob
And underground
Hid the nations lawmakers
An inch separating them

From pitchforks and guns

They said to themselves

The Caucasian politicians
We will get revenge
On the angry public

And on January 6
History was made
Not just because
It was my mom's birthday

The Caucasian politicians
Became very angry
Very upset
Because the threat to their life

They could not forget
On January 6
The politicians became mad
Forget the USS liberty

Forget the Tuskegee experiment
Forget the injustices
And recompense for slavery
The politicians were angry

And wanted revenge
And when they become that way
Nothing else matters
So, hearings began

Investigations planned
The kind that should have
Takin place
When JFK

Was assassinated

But when Israel moves
The truth runs and hides
9/11 testifies
But now

Only lies

Yes, the politicians are mad
When their lives are on the line
When White people outside
Rumbling and in full riot

Revenge we will get
Said the chickenshit lawmaker

No matter patriot American
The politicians are mad
And blood they will shed

When they feel violated

The mad politicians
Have an agenda
Justice for us
Rhetoric for you

The truth
Is a mighty weapon
In the hands of
The God of Abraham Isaac
And Jacob

this is the Israelites sonsoflight radio program. Before I begin, I want to give thanks to my Heavenly Father earthly mother, because of this incredible opportunity that I have to try to be a light and be a witness for the God of Abraham, Isaac and Jacob. That's my whole purpose for my creation. That is my whole agenda. You don't have to listen to many of my radio programs, to know the theme of what I talk about. My agenda is to be a fisher of men to the house of Israel to seek and save that which was lost, just like Messiah did. There is nothing else more important than to be about our father's business. This reality is solely for the purpose of testing your heart.

And what will you do? What are the true desires when you are faced with riches or you are faced with poverty? What decision will you make? Will you sow to the flesh or will you sew to the Spirit? Our nation is under a great vexation from the world from even our own nation from different spiritual pressures that we put on ourself in our nation, there is a trap sometimes in an unintentionally set by our own brethren. To make you think that we must do all things perfectly. Or none of it is any good when you are desiring to draw near to the God of Abraham, Isaac, and Jacob. No one even the strongest of us, the Hebrew Israelites, Negro, Latinos and Native Americans will worship perfectly will keep the commandments perfectly.

But from what I can see, when I read the scriptures is your heart and sincerity and truthfulness that matters in all things. Now, I named the title of the program tonight. "The truth will come out" the truth will come out to the great vexation of the world. I am speaking of the truth about the Hebrew Israelite. The 12 tribes of Israel the Negro, Latino and Native American on their father's side. The truth of the people of God will come out, the truth of the Hebrew Israelites will come out and the world will mourn. Why? Because of the long, long, long history of oppression, vexation, affliction, injustice, agendas that we have been subjected to all the years of our reality in the Western Hemisphere, and all over the world. The Hebrew Israelite 12 tribes of Israel, the truth will come out about who we are. And that is the single most terrible thing that the oppressor nations do not want to acknowledge. I want to say before I begin that I am an author and if you type in my name, Yaiquab Yisrael on Amazon. My books will come up. I also have a website twelvetribes Israelites.com, all lowercase lettering spelled together where you can go for ministry and information. And if the things I say resonate with you, then why don't you contact me? and let me talk to you and see if the room I have on Facebook called the Upper room, may be of service to you. My whole objective is to try to find that diamond in the rough who will seek to build up their foundation and hopefully, after having done so. Seek to do ministry to our nation to build them up, to pray for our nation and to edify our nation and if you feel you are not anointed to do ministry, then join me anyway. And let me share my gift with you to just try to minister to you on a daily basis. My gift of consistently faithfully sharing different scriptures and books that most likely you have not heard of, and most of which you have heard of, to try to help you to focus and to partake of daily bread.

That is my gift. That is what I have prayed for. And that is what my father who art in heaven has allowed me to do. My room is called the Upper room on Facebook. And that is me wearing the green and white garment. And I pray that you join us and let me try to minister unto you. I am a firm believer in using this reality to prepare for the eternal reality. The eternal kingdom of Abraham, Isaac and Jacob. That is my desire. I do not know when it began. But I know there are many brethren and sisters in our nation who are under the same anointing to love the word of the God of Abraham, Isaac and Jacob, you have the ability to see what this reality is all about.

We have evolved into a reality where the truth is no longer welcome. We realize that we are in a reality where the oppressor nations at the beginning, flat out took advantage of the curse we came under and took advantage of our labor of our lowly condition and evolved into a people where they oppress us more efficiently through their media, through their news through their political agendas. The oppressor nations, all have long all alone have sought to keep us ignorant. Not knowing that the Spirit of God cannot be constrained. That is the uphill battle. The oppressor nations have us to fight against us not knowing the truth will come out. The truth will win every single Iota, every single dotted I and crossed T will come to pass all that is hidden will be brought to light and there will be a recompence for all of the oppressors of the 12 tribes. Hebrew Israelites the Negro, Latino and Native American on their father's side. There will be a full recompense a double recompense as stated in Revelation against all, each and every one of the oppressors of the Hebrew Israelites.

Now, I want to say to the younger generation of Hebrews 30 and under I fear for you. I truly fear for you. Because the pull of the world I perceive affects you far more than the people of my generation. You are currently in a reality where depopulation is in full bloom you most likely have never heard of the Georgia Guidestones you have most likely never heard of Operation lockstep. You have most likely never heard of things like the Tuskegee experiment. You have most likely never heard of AIDS created to depopulate specifically our people, Negro, Latino, Native American. You, younger generation of Hebrew Israelites. You most likely do not know the depth of Satan. You most likely do not realize the agenda to probably completely wipe out the knowledge of the God of Abraham and Isaac and Jacob. You most likely will be unduly influenced by the media and those who own the media. Those who say they are Jews and our not, you younger generation of Hebrew Israelites more than likely have no other Israelite brethren to share with you the truth is not welcome in America anymore on platforms like YouTube, mainly or in the nationwide news media I know because when I try to call the local radio station here in the Bay Area, Kgo when I see an opportunity to be a light for our people, the Jewish talk show hosts will not let me speak a word once they find out what it is. I want to say. They have an agenda to stop the truth from coming out. That we are the Israelites. The Eternal Kingdom is ours. Judgment will be done and the children of Israel will be used by our Father who are in heaven to bring recompense, against, all who have oppressed us like Emmett Till, like Fred Hampton, like Breonna Taylor, like George Floyd, like Armaud Arbery like and all the other billions on top of brilliance. Did you hear what I said? I said billions of Hebrew Israelites who have had their blood spilled by our brother, Cain. The truth will come out. We do not have long to go. Every Sun rise announces 2024 is coming. It is at the doors. And even before then, as it says in First Thessalonians, we are not appointed to wrath you Hebrew Israelites, sons and daughters of light. Who minister who endure who commune with the angels, according to the Essene gospel of peace book four, you Hebrew Israelite sons and daughters of light who forsake the world who sow to the Spirit who know in your heart of hearts, the truth will come out, the truth of the God of Abraham Isaac, and Jacob will and must come out and when it comes out, America will be shown to be incredible. Incredible liars and condemned for the way she has used and abused the very people of God.

The nation states, led by America have now gotten themselves in a different kind of trouble. Using vaccinations as a way to make entry into the body to turn the body into source material to make the body subject to five G six G technology for the purpose of taking away your ability to think to feel or to resist the powers that be, to force you to make you do its bidding, a new type of evil to take a way you're freewill. Brothers and sisters. You will not hear my voice much longer. You will not hear big Judah much longer. You will not hear all likeminded brethren, much longer or sisters you will not hear the bride and the bride groom much longer. You will not hear the voice of those who endure of those who are a light in order to minister to you. They will have completed their work they will be called in from the field and because you did not come when the father call then you may have to go through the wine press of revelation 14 Where greater measures must be extracted to get you to fall down at the feet of the God of Abraham and Isaac and Jacob and produce the front which is worthy of repentance so that you may enter the eternal kingdom with shame on your forehead.

The bride and the bride groom will not be heard much longer. Brothers and sisters store up Redeem the time. Do not delay. I have a room on Facebook. It is a room for your benefit only, the truth will come out the secrets of our hearts will be revealed. Did we truly love our brethren to lay down our life for them? Do we truly love the angels? That the Essene gospel of peace tells us to commune with every day and night Essene gospel of peace book four our own benefit. While we are in this reality in a moment, in a twinkling of an eye we shall be changed for this corruption must put on this in- corruption and we will witness the marriage supper of the lamb and the tribulation of our oppressors who thought nothing of our labors who never thought the truth would come out, who patronized us and made us sing their national anthem. And even to this day, refuse to recompense for the Mid Atlantic slave trade. Brethren please, if anyone can hear me go to my website. twelvetribes israelites.com lowercase lettering all spelled together. Send me a message or get in contact with me or visit the website for ministry and information contact me on Facebook yaiquab Yisrael and allow me to talk to you to share with you what the room is about. I am looking for Hebrew Israelite sons and daughters of light who are lively stones and the word produces in effect out of you.

I want to give thanks to my Heavenly Father earthly mother for this incredible opportunity to join me Wednesday and Friday 8pm Until I see you again,

peace be unto you.

Shalom

Degrading further

I seem to recall a famous saying which is the more I learn the more I do not understand. As I read the spiritual books of antiquity, I have always tossed around in my mind a question, which is, why is it that the men of ancient civilizations seem to have more of a noble character than these current generations? There seems to be a chivalry and personal honor I see an ancient generation when I read the books dealing with previous generations. The common denominator that I seem to see is men governed by strict moral laws governing character. When I read the kolbrin Bible I seem to see the honor code among men in war, in communal relationships, and attitudes towards the elderly, in treating women with dignity and respect.

I even seem to get that sense in my spirit as recently as the early 1900s among the oppressor nations towards their own kind excluding, the 12 tribes of Israel the negro Latino and Native Americans, at least from my limited perspective, and the things I see by observing the sights and sounds and telecommunications and events of what the current reality has taught me. I once heard someone say the older men become the more advanced in their intellectual self but they become more corrupt as well. I realize I am in a time right now where I am witnessing the white man is actually destroying his only Kingdom. It seems he may have had lofty ideas for what it means to have a civilization at the start but it is amazing to me that this current reality has given way to outright lying and seem to trust in the ignorance of the common people to ever figure out the secret agendas they implement for world domination.

There is no is esteem anymore for personal character and accountability to the God of Abraham Isaac and Jacob. So, on we go having passed the point of no return a long time ago. It seems there is a cosmic decree handed down that the time of this civilization has reached its conclusion. The corruption in government and in the medical industry and its biological warfare and economic warfare is beyond comprehension that we would do the things we are doing to ourselves.

What I mean is engaging in be explicit warnings of Matthew chapter 24 without fear or concern. This is quite amazing to me that we have no sense of personal accountability as we see the leaders that be in America continuing to only engage in infighting politically and have given themselves over to outright lies about what is going on between Ukraine and Russia at the present and lying about the reason why the conflagration started.

There is an insane logic that America seems to think that if they lie about the truth, it will somehow change the fate of what the spirit of God says must come to pass. It would be better if America instead of singing the national anthem would pray out loud Psalm 23. But we cannot because we are too far gone in corruption and love of money and conquest and carnal living to change. It is an amazing thing to see America consistently give billions of dollars through the Ukraine instead of two its own nation suffering from food shortage and economic calamity. Truly I have learned a lesson about what happens when a nation sacrifices its moral character for short term advantage.

I am amazed

truly

ode woe

a great many people
I saw and wondered
Within myself
Is it really possible?

The only God
Are themselves?
I do not mean
To be nosey

But try as I may
I cannot escape
The vanity of all things
Captured by what is temporary

Is it really true?
Only the here and now
All that matters
In life?

America, I feel for you
So touchy
So thin skinned
Easily offended

A result of…
The matriarchal family

So there
You get what you deserve

And now
Paying a price
With no end in sight
Just a generation

After generation
After generation

Of the new man
Created after

His selfish mind
Putting God on defense
Why did you create me?
Thus?
Says he
To himself

America this is you
Thoroughly corrupted
Because of great blessings
We felt we were due

And now the world watches
Our skirts are lifted
Our corruption manifested
We say one thing

But do the opposite

And worst of all
You make the children of Israel
Negro Latino and native American
Sing the national anthem

The very song
Of our oppressors

That is why
You cannot go on
Instead of singing praises
To the God of our father

You love playing the whore

Every whore
Gets old
And needed no more

And castaway

Her children forgotten
Her history written
The new generation
Unfit and dying

July 5th

Happy birthday Lionel

July 6th 2022

Happy birthday chuck

August 11th 2019

Goodbye dad

Goodbye mom

Testy pt3

And hello and thank you for joining me. My name is Yaiquab Yisrael. And this is the Israelites sons of Light radio program. And before I begin, I want to give thanks to my Heavenly Father and my earthly mother. For this absolutely incredible opportunity I have to redeem the time to store up treasure while I am in this reality. Anyone who was listening, I want to let you know that if anything I say resonates with you. I have a website called twelvetribesisraelites.com lowercase lettering all spelled together for ministry and information. I have a room on Facebook called the upper room where I use my gift to share verses consistently from books you have probably never heard of, books you have not heard of, in an effort to help you endure this reality and to be about our Father's business and hopefully, to help you gain a vision to use your gift to minister to the nation of Israel. Negros Latinos and Native Americans. Before I begin, I want to let you know the title of the program tonight." Testify pt. three".

Every now and then Spirit comes on me to give praise to the Heavenly Father because of the abundance of all things that I have received and have received and will continue to receive. So much so that I do not have room for, the blessings that continue to be bestowed upon me on a daily basis. And so tonight, I wanted to give praise and halalyah not Hallelujah. Hallelujah means praise not. Yah. It's one of the devices of the gods of this world to keep you from giving proper praise, honor and glory to our Father who art in heaven halalyah means praise yah, Halayah and I'm really thrilled to convey that information to you. Because we, the Hebrew Israelites, naturally want to praise and worship Our Father who art in heaven the right way. But there are many things that are taught to us that are in error and we are in the time of our enlightening and that was one of the things that I recently learned. So, I am thrilled to be able to share it with you now. Also, before I begin, I wanted to say as I always do, I am a fisher of men, Hebrew Israelite sons and daughters of light. brethren and sisters, who have an anointing on their soul to draw near, one way or another, to the God of Abraham, Isaac, and Jacob I am one of your brothers. I am with you. I have my room on Facebook, where I dedicate myself to posting and sharing information about events on the horizon that I think may apply to our nation. I consider myself a family dog in the sense that I will start barking, if any information that comes to my attention from the oppressor nations, whom the Heavenly Father, if you read Psalm 64 is making their own tongue fall upon them, and they are spilling the beans on the demise of their own kingdom.

We only have a few months left until April 2024. And I say halalyah, every new sunrise represents one day less for the Hebrew Israelites to remain in our captivity. Now I also want to say every now and in YouTube bans me and suspends me, make a note of the link in my description box on bitchute. Because when you see me and I have not been posting for a few days, then you know I was suspended but when I upload to bitchute, brother I let it all hang out. It's one of the last platforms that seem to let you say what you truly feel so when you see I haven't been posting. You know what happened to me. Or in case I am afflicted and have to stay in the hospital. As happens to me from time to time. Since I am in an afflicted body.

Now, something happened to me last week or maybe two weeks ago and I have to say it might be the biggest miracle blessing I have ever seen in my life. At the time I was suspended and I uploaded my testimony to bitchute. Now I want to do the same thing on YouTube. Now I believe a son or daughter of light should have a testimony of the things that you have been blessed with in your reality for the good or the bad. A testimony is something that you can share, to help brethren learn a lesson either way, for the good or for the bad. Now this particular testimony that I am ready to share happened a week or two ago.

I had a chance to do a little ministry to some people. And I have been blessed with the opportunity to minister one way or another. Since I have been called into ministry about 11 or 12 years ago and there have been many blessings I have received and still received to this day because of the opportunity to minister when the cry for charity goes out, now even still the evil spirit counterfeit spirit within my soul at the first cry of charity rebels and does not want to give, that is why I give thanks for the opportunity to give because anytime there is an opportunity to burn your flesh, you must take advantage of it. That is what putting the flesh to death is it is the same thing as purifying your soul. That is the only way that we can produce fruit that is profitable for our enduring this world and our own counterfeit spirit that tends to drive us to evil thinking evil actions, evil results.

Now I was able to minister and I thought nothing of it. And for some reason I had the thought in my mind to look for a vehicle that I wanted because, the present vehicle that I had, was insufficient for me because I am a brother who is bound for the time being to a powerchair and electric wheelchair and I have been for the past four years. It is part of my blessing. So, for the time being I am restricted so I am able to commit to ministry. The opportunity came along and I ministered to the sister and the Spirit came upon me to consider what vehicle I'm looking for. Consider the vehicle I really wanted because the vehicle I had at that time was hard for me to drive because of having to shift having to brake having to clutch in having to drive and I cannot move my legs as fast as I want to making me a danger to myself and to the public. So, I began to look for an automatic that it would be easier for me to drive now consider this was two days after I was able to do ministry, which blessed my soul in itself because I know the way to receiving is giving now, I looked at a vehicle. I had no faith that I would possess the vehicle I looked at and when I set my heart on something I plan to have in the far-off future. Do you know that four hours later I was sitting in it?

 I repeat I had a small chance to minister I thought nothing of it. The Spirit came upon me to look at a vehicle I would like to have. I chose one not believing I would have it until I saved up and probably would be ready to receive it next year at the earliest and do you know three or four hours later, I was sitting in my own vehicle the vehicle I desired. I was in possession of only four or three hours later, brethren. Now I didn't have the reaction. That I thought I might have of joy and incredible unbelief. I was rather subdued at this miracle that had just taken place. I was very, very full of praise and thanksgiving. Don't get me wrong. I lit incense all day, gave praise and halalyah to My Father who art in heaven and blessed his holy name but inside of me deep inside of me. I did not have the reaction that I thought I would have because of the time we are living in. We are living in such a serious time. And I know that this is the time that I personally have been waiting for ever since I started doing ministry.

I want to say to anyone who is listening the time is coming. You will not hear voices like big Judah. Abdullah seer adir Bay Israel. Big Levi and all the brothers who are ministering to you rawdaph Bey Israel. All these brothers and sisters do you know we are ready to leave the Earth? That is why my reaction to receiving the vehicle that I wanted was subdued. It seemed as if everybody who saw my new vehicle was happier than I was at having been able to purchase it but I know there are bigger issues going on right now that are so serious. And I pray does not come upon our nation. But I fear that there is great trouble coming upon our own nation of brothers and sisters who are filled with the spirit of apathy.

Brethren, I fear for what is on the horizon for our nation. Our brethren our sisters after all we have been through so my reaction was subdued for the last 10 or 11 or 12 years since I have been ministering all that time. I have walked around with a broken heart for my nation for the different vicissitudes of life. The attacks of the gods of this world against brethren like myself and my other ministering brethren My heart has been broken this whole time because I know that the wine press of revelation 14 is at the door. The wine press of revelation 14 The Great Tribulation the day of the Lord, the wrath of God. The trouble is already brewing. I spoke of a possible God event April 24 of this year. I pray for an explosion like our nation, our whole nation. The good and the evil to be miraculously transformed and our captivity finish. It did not come to pass but there was an earthquake that most of us more than likely did not hear about, our old buddy Israel. turn their back on the United States dollar. They will not trade in the dollar any more. And these are the people who own the Federal Reserve. This action will cause the dollar to be greatly devalued at a time where the seal of Revelation six verse three. The rider on the Black Horse is now riding. The scales in his hand are financial reset. The pronouncement the rider of Revelation chapter six verse three was a denarius for a quart of wheat and three pennies for a quart of barley and hurt not the oil and the wine. I confess I do not have the overstanding of hurt not the oil and the wine. It could possibly conjecture the elite will not be hurt by the inflation of the world of the gas prices of the world of the food shortage of the world. The dainties of this life but the 99% of the world will suffer until the wrath of God falls at which time the whole world bar none, will experience nuclear war which in my humble opinion is the wrath of God. I seem to see in this present reality the seeds of pre wrath. I have been looking at various videos of the oppressors warning us of things that are soon to come that harmonize with Revelation chapter six verse three. So, because of all these things with the miracle that happened to me a couple of days ago being able to purchase the van that I wanted the reason for my reaction was not what it should have been because of the confluence of events we are heading into and I perceive we are not prepared.

I perceive that our nation for the most part is not Redeeming the time. We are still singing the other nations national anthem if you have been watching the NBA championships, even till the last day, our oppressors will not stop patronizing us and making a fool out of us. In making us sing their songs. If I may digress for a moment, I am willing to wager that for the next two NBA games they will most likely have Hebrew Israelites. Either a man or a woman sings the national anthem as they have, I believe the other five games, Hebrew Israelites singing the oppressor's national anthem. These are the very people who are not ready for the winepress instead. of singing or reciting Psalm 23. Our oppressors make us sing their song.

Do you see why I've carried around a broken heart all of these years? do you see why my reaction? Although I am thankful for the miracle that happened to me. And I could go on and on and on and testify. Anyone who is drawing near without a testimony, I am very suspect of you, you should not be able to hold in the blessings of the Heavenly Father.

Join me in my room on Facebook called the Upper Room. Send me a friend invite. Let's Redeem the time together. Want to give thanks to my Heavenly Father earthly mother for this incredible opportunity.

And until I see you again. peace be unto you

shalom

belinda

things would be a whole lot easier on me if I just knew how to control my spirit. The conversation went like this, she said hello to me I said I would appreciate it if you do not speak to me, she said why? I said because you are stupid and a flatterer and I cannot stand flatterers. Even after those incredibly harsh words she tried to persist to talk to me. I wish I wouldn't be so harsh sometimes I wish I wouldn't be so thin skinned sometimes I wish I was better able to accept human foibles then I currently do. I may never graduate to the fully spiritual realm of people who know how to accept peoples faults far better than me. I wish I could learn the secret of life is to love people unconditionally and to realize that everyone is made in the image of God. I wish I would learn that in this current reality we are a world of broken spirits including myself so why is it that sometimes I act as if I am the only one who is 100% normal? Sometimes I really tickle myself to death with the things I do and the things I think. The psychological and mental maladies of the human condition convinces me more than anything that the supreme spirit the God of Abraham Isaac and Jacob does exist. All forms testify to the reality of the God of the Hebrews. I think once I learn the lesson of accepting human weakness, I will be well on my way to knowing who the God of the Israelites is.

I'm sorry Belinda

I pray a healing for you spiritually and mentally

Help me God

"The earth is the Lords and the folders thereof" Psalm 24 1

To me that helps explain why all of a sudden out of the blue I was gifted with a new minivan simply because I had the opportunity to minister charity to two sisters in need. One thing that thrills my soul is watching how the God of Abraham Isaac and Jacob have worked in my life. Without a shadow of a doubt, I have seen incredible things happen to me good and evil. The earth is the Lords and the fullness thereof the glory of God covers the whole earth in my life over and over again the God of Abraham Isaac and Jacob has assured me that he will make a way for me to overcome in faith while I am in this reality and that is truly been amazing to me. I have been able to minister charity two brethren in need for a few years now. I understand that the way to receiving is to give sincerely and from your heart. And now I am testifying of having been given the opportunity to share to some sisters in need and all of a sudden, a couple of days later I am sitting in a minivan that I desperately needed because of my disabled condition. I doubt if a man without a testimony knows the God of Abraham Isaac and Jacob truthfully. If he calls the negroe Latino and Native American on their father's side children are the fathers of this world better to their children than the God of all creation? Absolutely not and this is what I am finding out as I live out my reality. People always say I am blessed but I can say I can prove it.

contemplation

It's kind of a shame that I had to be as lonely as I am companionship wise but it had to be that way, I understand that now. It seems that the highest level of success along the way involves a great degree of loneliness. Companionship wise significant loneliness can be a crushing Crucible to the soul, but I understand the fruit it bears when it is under the proper influences. I realize that all things ultimately come from the God of spirits, the God of Abraham Isaac and Jacob and I also realize that I am in a fallen reality with everyone playing their part, most of the time not to their satisfaction at what they're called to do and what they're called to be. But I find that is not me, I find that I am unimaginably thrilled at who I am called to be and what I am called to do. Many times, I just cannot believe my good fortune at having been elected to believe in the God of Abraham Isaac and Jacob and then spend my time testifying and ministering to his glory. I know that many people are condemned when I began to testify of my faith and works. I do not mean to offend anyone but I realize that we are elected to do what we do, whether it is faith and works or unbelief and apathy. I believe every man has free will to decide the path he will go down. I believe through reasoning and intellect the God of Abraham Isaac and Jacob can be found. But I find again in this reality there is little solace in having been called to a life of great loneliness and isolation. But the reward is above the highest of highest. And I am satisfied with my calling.

Slow goodbye to Esau and Japheth

Thank you for joining me. My name is yaiquab ban yisrael. And this is the Hebrew Israelite sons of light radio program. I can't thank you enough for joining me. Before I begin, I want to give thanks to my heavenly Father, earthly mother for this incredible, great opportunity that they have given to me to be a light while I am in this reality, to use my life to be the best witness I can for the reality of the God of Abraham, Isaac, and Jacob. I want to say to anyone listening that I am a fisher of men and women lively stone, Hebrew Israelites. Who desire to store up while you are in this reality, to redeem the time by taking your mental spiritual physical energies and devote as much as you can to the Ministry of our nation, the Negro, Latino and Native Americans on your father's side, better known as the children of Israel, the 12 tribes of Israel.

I want to say that I have a ministry. I have a website I have a room on Facebook called the upper room. You will see my icon the white garment and green garment I have a website twelvetribesisraelites.com lowercase lettering all spelled together. I invite you to visit either one of those send me a friend invite on Facebook or you can get in contact with me on the website twelvetribes israelites.com I wanted to name the title of the program tonight. "Slow goodbye to Esau and Japheth" I cannot say who Japheth is because I will be banned. So, I leave it up to you to know who I am referring to when I use Japheth the first letter is correct. And the last letter is "h" so please try to keep that in mind as I do my programs.

Slow goodbye to Esau and Japheth. Esau being the Caucasian both are the historical enemies of Israel, the Negro, Latino and Native American. I want to use this program to say goodbye to Esau and Japheth. I want to say goodbye to the raping of our women that you have done and the murdering of our children that you have done. I want to say goodbye to your slavery that you have done to us and the Mid Atlantic slave trade even till now. For your patronizing of the Negro, Latino and Native American. I want to say goodbye for George Floyd for Emmitt till for Nat Turner for Breonna Taylor for Armaud Arbury I want to say goodbye for Martin Luther King and the endless lists of Hebrew Israelites that you have lynched that you have murdered and ignored the cries of the mothers who cried bitterly and there was no power in the hand of the Hebrew Israelite men to adequately recompense you for the things that you have done unto us for the destruction of our family, for the hidden experimental agendas to depopulate us, we want to say goodbye to your Christianity and Catholicism, and we say goodbye to your racial and institutional racism, we want to say goodbye to your jails and prisons, to your justice system.

Your educational system for making us sing, your national anthem your you're banking policies towards the children of Israel and disregarding our labor and stealing from us and your unequal application of the law that you have committed against us for the theft of our homes and property. We say goodbye for the slander of the God of our fathers. Goodbye, Esau and Japheth. Say goodbye to all these things that you have done unto us and more can you blame us?

 But say hello Esau and Japheth to slavery and bondage to the Hebrew Israelites. The 12 tribes of Israel say hello to the Negro the Latino and the Native American at whose feet you will bow at whose feet you will serve and for recompense for all the things that you have done unto us. Say hello to receiving double for all that you have done for lying to us for the sake of advantage when we were in our weakness and could not defend ourselves against your hatred, your murderous bloodletting and inveigling our minds just like it says in the Book of Jasher Chapter 28 Verse 20. Say hello to constant pain of heart and grief and recompense and the wrath of the God of Abraham, Isaac, and Jacob,

 Say hello to the eternal kingdom in which Hebrew Israelite men and women will sing for joy of heart because of the abundance of all things which Our Father who art in heaven will give unto us as if a father in this current reality would give to his children. Psalm 34 7 "says that he will give us the desire of our hearts". The prayer of our fathers has gone up to the ears of sabboath and he have heard us and he have restored our overstanding and we are waking up and every day we awaken more and more. The Hebrew Israelite sons of light are bringing more light to our nation and strengthening our nation to leave your reality of sin and iniquity and your politics and your love of blood and love of filthy lucre and the Israelites are leaving as we watch your kingdom suffer under its own weight.

Every new sunrise brings us closer to 2024 April fifth, when a great phenomenon will take place and no one will be able to deny the "x" that will appear over America and the whole world will witness it. Whether or not the 12 tribes will be here. I do not know whether or not it means the beginning of Jacob's trouble. The Great Tribulation. I do not know. I tend to think that it is the end of something. X means finished. "X" means done with "x" means stop. "X" means no more.

Every new sunrise means we are one day closer to the end of this damnable reality that is called American. Brethren, let me digress for a moment and repeat something that I want to say that I want to try to remember to remind us from now on the word Hallelujah means "praise not Yah". Hallelujah means praise, not yah. It is better to say halalyah, which means praise Yah. It's one of the ways that the powers that be the gods of this world, seek to blemish our worship of the god of Abraham, Isaac and Jacob a Hebrew Israelite spiritual son and daughter of life is the most powerful force on the face of the earth. It has now occurred to me that the reasons why we have gone through in our reality the things that we have gone through is so that the oppressor nations can build an irrefutable case against themselves. For the sake of righteous judgment. When you research the timelines that point to the end of our captivity, you will quickly see that we have come to the end of the timelines as we know it.

Now, I could be wrong and there may be new information that comes out that points to a more imminent deliverance of our nation. Then we knew of before I also want to repeat that to the best of my overstanding. The Scripture says we… we, you Hebrew Israelite. Sons and Daughters of light are not appointed to wrath. First Thessalonians five. We should commit this thing to memory brethren and sisters because of the confluence of events in the world today. I have been speaking of Revelation Chapter Six verse three, most recently with great assurance that we are in the time of the opening of the third seal without a shadow of a doubt.

It speaks of massive death it speaks of a financial reset. It speaks of great inflation and food shortage. Has anyone heard that at the present time Spending for an average American family is $490 more a month on food? how do you think that affects the Hebrew Israelites? We have historically struggled economically to feed our families and our brethren and sisters. And I want to say right now, if anyone is listening to me and you are suffering food insecurity or you know a sister with children who is suffering from food insecurity. I want to say that please contact me and I will do the best I can to help you. I will not run from you. I will not put it off to try to help you. I am only one brother, but I will do my level best to help you.

And I pray that anyone listening to the sound of my voice join with me and send me your email. And if I get a call for charity in your state that I can direct them to you. My dream is to have four or five brethren for each state. Spread out so that when the cry for charity goes out, our whole nation can pitch in if we come to the time of great famine and food shortage in our own nation, that we can minister to each other so that we may minister to our own and through prayer and supplication we will minister to our own brothers and sisters especially sisters with children and no spouse to help deliver her economically. Then we will do it ourselves.

You can contact me at Israelite 94 yahoo.com and simply tell me where you live. And that you are volunteering to minister and if I get a cry for charity in your area, I will contact you and you can take it upon yourself to help the brother or sister. Again, my email is Israelite94@yahoo.com and let me know your state and city so that I can organize different brethren in the United States to minister to unfortunate Hebrew Israelites. If the cry for charity goes out.

 Does anybody know who John Boyd Jr. is? He is a member of the Negro Farmers Association. If I'm not mistaken, he may very well be the head of the Negro Farmers Association. Now, I recently saw him on TV. give witness predicting the worst is yet to come. For food shortage. The brother is another very credible witness for Revelation Chapter Six agriculturally happening right now in our face.

Brethren, we are at a time where we should drop everything and do whatever we can to store up and redeem the time so that we may be found worthy to escape the things coming on the earth. Did you brethren know that scientists have created robots with robotic skin has anyone heard that? Robots have been created that have feelings? Robots with the minds of eight nine-year-olds. I recently heard a video where the scientists mentioned they have created a robot that is able to reason with human beings and express emotion such as fear of being turned off. Now I tend to believe that this is the case. Now Esau lies so much. You don't know what to believe sometimes. But with the advances in science as it is I tend to see the credibility in these things. Brethren, I've run out of time. I want to give thanks to my heavenly Father, my earthly mother, etc. Contact me on Facebook where I will simply seek to minister to you by way of Scripture posting. I buy books so that I may bring the over standing of what I believe are faithful books to your attention. Books that you have most likely not heard of. So let me minister unto you, to help you to run from this kingdom as fast and far away as you can and to endure for the soon restoration of the Hebrew Israelites

want to give thanks to my Heavenly Father earthly mother for this incredible opportunity.

Please join me Wednesday and Friday at 8pm on the Israelite sons of like radio program. And until I see you again

Shalom

Almost everyday

This is something I have to make sure I put down for memory's sake in my book. The other day I went to sell something on eBay. I was soon contacted by yet another person trying to scam me. This caused me to sit back for a moment and to think about what I have been coming across in my life for at least the past couple of years people wise. It is a sad commentary on the declining character values of people in my humble opinion so far is my current reality is concerned. It seems as if the vast majority of people I am coming across have some ulterior motive in mind to defraud me usually of money one way or another. People do not seem to realize that when you carry this type of spirit in you, of sin and iniquity it works against you so that you can never succeed and you will always be in need of defrauding others. I am truly amazed at observing this in people over and over and over again or is it that I look like a human lollipop, a sucker for people to lick? I have learned that spiritually you grow by observing people who have no need of the spirit and have No Fear of the God of Abraham Isaac and Jacob. There is much to be learned from these types of people and the power of the counterfeit spirit. In this day and age in America people have turned to simply trying to survive. Many people have not set themselves up to live in a stable environment as they approach middle age and old age. I do not believe all people are evil hearted but their situation is such that it has driven them to desperate measures in order to survive one more day. There is no inclination in man's world to cry out to the God of Abraham Isaac and Jacob. Each transgression leads further and further down the rabbit hole of desperation and defrauding others. A spiritual man will take note of these things and adjust his thinking so that this same fate may not come upon him. This I have learned to do from a young age and it makes me realize how truly blessed I am to have gone down this path of fearing the God of Abraham Isaac and Jacob and this has kept me from the people I have observed who must turn to illicit means to live.

Truth and pain

The future is truth
And it is coming
It is on its way
There is no stopping truth

The world knows
it must come
Much hurt is involved
Before healing can be

The truth
Must have its day
There will be pain
It is already here

To live
More expensive
By the minute
By the second

The life we knew
No longer
Compatible with the truth
Only lies

Because the powers
That be
No that
A reckoning has come

And the life
Of the flesh
Has run its course
Now only the spirit

Really matters
The eternal spirit
Of life

In God our father

The truth must come
That life is
Majority vanity
The truth has come

It brings much pain
The truth brings
A sour testimony
It is very bitter indeed

With ourselves
We must confess
No more
Fake appearances

All is manifest
Our strengths and weaknesses
And pride
To be weighed in the balances

The truth must come
Pain will follow
The pain of hiding
What is real

For ego

A healing will follow
To bless our soul
And destroyed the works
Of the devil

To make truth a friend
To be honest with ourselves
Is to make our father
A friend

To lift us

On high
To love the truth
In all things

Even when
The truth hurts
to produce a fruit
of righteousness

Our saving grace
All mankind

A vortex

The warnings coming out of Europe can barely be believed. For some reason Europe and America seem to want to know what a world nuclear war looks like in Russia keeps coming down on the right side of history destroying American funded biological weapons labs in Eastern Europe mainly the Ukraine which is what the current hostilities between Russia and Ukraine are all about. The world stands by knowing in their heart that they are headed for a global cosmic chastisement like no other. The feeling that is in the air reminds me of when I knew that I was going to get a spanking from my dad. My only thought was to hurry and get it over with. But with this situation there is no getting over it, this thing is from the God of Abraham Isaac and Jacob the current world situation has become a downward spiral. There is this strange desire to provoke Russia because The United States sees Russia as a threat standing in the way too global dominion. The people are not too concerned as long as the paychecks come and the dainties flow. Or is it that we are under a mass hypnosis knowing what is to come yet living in denial until the very last second. There is no conversation communication in the mainstream media that people should prepare to meet the God of Abraham Isaac and Jacob. There is no one who can take heat two sound logic and good reasoning of compromise. The love of money and power has given birth to corruption on a level that is beyond the mental faculties of this present reality. The evil is spiritual it testifies of the fall of Satan it testifies of his promise to give the world to anyone who would worship him in the book of Matthew chapter 4. The people sit and wait the stage is set we will not overcome the current reality and prosper I am convinced.

Rick and Rothschild

1913
Federal Reserve
FBI
IRS

The year
they were created

The reserve to print
FBI to punish
IRS to tax

The Jews
All together
Sitting in a room
Jekyll island

Let's give em something
That's what they said
Gotta figure out a way
Call it central bank

To print money
Then charge usury
What a winning ticket
They said to themselves

We will use
Gentile puppets
To institute
debt enslavement

We will take
Advantage of
Their greed and lust
For money

President and politician

It don't matter to me
Rothschild said
I own the money
So, tell the elite

kiss
My ass

And then
2 donkeys
Came together
And gave birth

To a son
They named
Rick Dick Nixon
He kissed
Rothschilds ass

Just give me money
Rick dick said
And I'll do anything
You say

So, Rothschild said
I have a cousin
His name is Fiat
It means nothing
Worthless
Paper

And I want you
To make him king

Rick said
I have an idea
And Rothschild listened
Money for nothing

I like it I like it
Rothschild said
So, rick dick
Erased the gold standard

Just trust us
We will pay it back
After all
We are the United states

Of America

And Fiat grew and grew
And gold never came back

Fiat money
Good for nothing
Strangling a country
Amazing thing

Then gold came calling
And Fiat had nothing
Down came a country
Sad story

No way

It seems like for the one millionth time it is really really true and still I refuse to believe it. Are there really people in the world who traffic in children? Who performed satanic rituals on children? Is this really true? I refuse to believe it but I keep hearing about it but in my gut I perceive that there are people in the world who are really this deranged. I do not want to acknowledge it at all. When I see a child's face on TV I turn away. Because I do not have the strength to look into their innocent eyes. And in addition, my blood begins to boil at the thought of this type of thing going on. Yet over and over again when I turned to the left and when I turned to the right there is a missing child here a dead child there and abused child over there. That is why I crave leaving this reality. Even if there is only one child out of a trillion who must suffer at the perverted minds and hearts of grown adults then the whole world should not be able to go on. I know in my heart the God of Abraham Isaac and Jacob well fully recompense children I believe that with all my heart. Until that time comes, I will say to myself these things are not really happening it is only an illusion never ever can nice things be true of these things happening to children and in this way, I expect to hold onto my sanity.

The jig is up pt2

And hello, thank you for joining me. My name is yaiquab ban yisrael. And this is the Israelite sons of flight radio program which I try to do every Wednesday and Friday at 8pm pst. In an effort to redeem the time to store up treasure in preparation for the eternal kingdom. I want to give thanks to my heavenly father, and my earthly mother for this incredible opportunity that I have to be a light to my nation, the Hebrew Israelites you Negros, Latinos and Native Americans. On your father's side, you are the Hebrew Israelites and my ministry is for you. It is about you. It is to you and I am here to say that if ever, there was a time that you should draw nearer to the God of Abraham, Isaac, and Jacob. Then brother now, right now is the time and I kid you not, if you can somehow overstand the time you are living in then you should know now, absolutely. Right now is the time to seek out your spiritual self, to know the God of Abraham Isaac and Jacob while you have the opportunity.

I am a fisher of men and women light brethren, who have a spiritual passion who meditate on spiritual things. The God of Abraham, Isaac, Jacob the things of the Bible, the things of the Nag Hammadi. The things of the apocryphal books for brethren who have a spiritual hunger who must feed on the Word of God in order to live. My ministry is for you. I have a room on Facebook. You are invited. All you have to bring is a willingness to learn, to be fed, to share things that are a part of your reality. With other brethren to participate and to realize that this is our opportunity to write our eternal witness for the future kingdom of the Negro, the Hebrew Israelites.

 Now, brethren, I entitled The name of the program, "the jig is up". "The jig is up" I am a brother, who constantly looks at the events of the world because I am anxiously awaiting the restoration of our people, the twelvetribesisraelites.com. I have a website that you can visit if you want to get in touch with me. all lowercase lettering spelled together, you can contact me for ministry and information. I also want to let the nation know that I want to establish a nationwide ministry whereby we can take care of our destitute brothers and sisters especially sisters with children. And what I mean by that is if you want to be a part of such a ministry, please contact me at Israelite 94@yahoo.com I am trying to gather a list of brethren spread out across the United States who want to volunteer to be called upon in case the cry for charity goes out and you are able to minister to someone close by you and I want to encourage brethren who have greater ministries to do the same in an effort to minister to our own kind.

Brethren, the jig is up. The jig is finish, the jig was our captivity. The jig is up if you are paying attention to the events of the world. It should be very obvious that we are in a time that we have never seen before by far. Now you know that I cannot be too specific in talking about the details of what I mean. And the people who are behind the agendas that we are currently under or I will be suspended for a week or two weeks or six months. That is one way you know that we are in a time of great evil when you are not even allowed to speak your mind. And let me say right now if you come on my channel and I have not posted anything. Then you know I came under the hook. I like to post every single night scriptures that may help a brother or sister to endure the current reality at least one more day. That is the important thing for our nation to bear fruit to minister if you can and to continue in faith as we see the day drawing near. The jig is truly up.

Brethren when you look at the confluence of videos and alternative media, where most of the truth tellers are you will see there is a judgment in the land that will lead to the day of the Lord and the wrath of God. Nuclear war if you look at the media, the topics will be the vaccination program the war and Russia the economy, the food shortage, the gas shortage, transgenderism in other words you will see Revelation chapter six verse three and on... the agenda is becoming clearer and clearer. The plan is the destruction of America because fiat currency is no longer trading with other nations, the other nations do not want fiat currency. The dollar is losing its value. And when that happens, when other nations do not want to play along and continue trading in worthless money, then brother we have to go to war and that is what you see right now in the Ukraine. nations of the world are not trading in the petro dollar anymore. America was using Ukraine to launder money. In other words, we send it to them and they kick us back a little bit of the action the jig is up. Nations are pegging their money to commodities. Gold and silver and dropping the dollar that is why we are sending billions of dollars to Ukraine. Because if the Ukraine collapses the jig will truly be up. And Russia every day is gaining a little more ground and the powers that be are trying to figure out how to get out of the situation.

And Russia is no longer interested in negotiating. Russia is showing itself to be on the right side of history. They said they want to put an end to the Bio Labs that many of you have not heard of. You do not know about. Russia said these Bio Labs were backed by the United States and that their purpose is to create a virus that will depopulate Russian people now there is a woman a virologist, a Ph. D. That you can go online and listen to any of her videos. Now her name is Dr. Judy Mikovits,and she will tell you that the virus called aids that was a big deal in the late 80s and 90s. was for the purpose of depopulating the children of Israel now she did not mention the Negro or Latino or the Native Americans. But she did mention so called "Black people" so called" Indian people". She stated that virus was created for us which is no surprise.

We should know by now that Psalm 83 is true. And the conspiracy of the nations the truth is coming out about who we are and the powers that be don't like it and they are doing something about it. Number one they are trying to eliminate the knowledge of the God of Abraham, Isaac and Jacob two they are trying to institute the worship of Satan. Matthew chapter four (check). They are about to implement programs that will force you to comply by way of social credit score like they have in China. Let's say you want to take the bus to work. But there's one problem your social score must be 650 or higher. to board this bus and if your score your social credit score is lower. Then you cannot board the bus until you comply with any of the myriad of programs that they will force you to do to earn points.

 Now I could be wrong. But with all the agendas in the world today. There is one of two reasons for the purpose of them, depopulation and forced compliance to the powers that be. Matthew Chapter Four all these things will I give you said Satan to Messiah. If you fall down and worship me, brethren, the agenda of the world is forced compliance to do the will of the powers that be, if you do not want to comply then maybe you will not be allowed to eat for two days.

Forced compliance by way of food shortages. And that is just one of the ways to make the people comply that I see on the horizon. Brethren, allow me to say this I am a brother who is a firm believer in not wasting any time No, not even one second. When it comes to building your testimony and preparing yourself at the present time. For the time when we must give an account of our selves. I am a firm believer of not wasting any time at all to build a testimony which is written in heaven. You don't have to be perfect to minister I am a perfect example of that the fact that you are not called to be perfectly able to minister, you can still be a son or daughter of light.

The current reality is for you to write your testimony. That's why I have a room on Facebook called the upper room where I try to minister to help you to do ministry. Brethren, join me and my brethren and redeem the time while we have time. Allow me to digress for a moment and speak about soon coming explosive issues in a couple of days that may come to pass.

Now the Supreme Court is going to make a decision on the legality of abortion. And there are opposition groups promising an explosion if abortion Roe vs. Wade is over turn. Did anyone see the video of all those dead cows in Kansas? Do you think this is what biological warfare looks like? Has anyone seen the video of all those diesel semi-trucks parked on the side of the road? Because there was no more diesel at the truck stops?. Did anyone see that? The main stream media is not very good at showing you these types of things.

They are not very good at showing you what the Negro farmer whose name is John boyd of the Negro Farmers Association and the warning that he put out about this fall we are going to feel it. When you look at the oppressor nations, they place their redemption in storing up in buying guns and ammo and digging a hole in the ground to wait it out. Never ever will they cry out to the God of Abraham, Isaac and Jacob. Oh, you might hear them throw God a bone and talk about how they are Christians. But we know that the oppressor nations view christianity as fire insurance.

Brethren behold the defeat and downfall of those who have oppressed us. They know not why these things have come upon them. They have no clue. That is because of the Mid Atlantic slave trade. That is because of our brothers and sisters who were lynched. They have no clue why these things are coming upon them because they took advantage of our labor. And worst yet, the Hebrew Israelites will walk away with the riches of the world and they know none of these things. The old presser nations they do not know how to cry out. Second to the God of Abraham, Isaac, and Jacob. Did anyone see the Pfizer document that showed that women who got the shot in the first trimester miscarry 80 to 82% of the time. Second, brethren, there is so many problems and hotspots in the world. Today. If you are a Hebrew, Israelite and you do not believe in the God of Abraham, Isaac and Jacob I don't want to be rude. But you have got to be crazy.

I want to give thanks to my Heavenly Father earthly mother for this spreadable opportunity.
Please join me Wednesday and Friday at 8pm. And until I see you again, peace be unto you,
Shalom.

A mystery

"Now these are the foods with which the devil lies in wait for us. First he injects a pain into your heart until you have heartache on account of a small thing of this life, and he seizes (you) with his poisons. And afterward (he injects) the desire of a tunic, so that you will pride yourself in it, and love of money, pride, vanity, envy that rivals another envy, beauty of body, fraudulence. The greatest of all these are ignorance and ease."

The authoritative discourse
the nag Hammadi

ptsd

yet another
Psychological malady
PTSD
Rearing its head
Almost daily

In the life of
my neighbor
And good friend
Remnants of

Memories
Of times past

Back and forth he goes
Washing and waxing
A spot not there
Yet still

Washing and waxing
PTSD
Keeps you busy
For sanity's sake

To erase the memories
Of weapons and war
Loud noises and bombs
Day and night

PTSD
Discriminates not
An agent of the devil
In the hearts and minds

Of those who fought
And those who died
Ravaging the soul
With memories

Born of nightmares
United States military
And veterans
Of all nationalities

He washed his car
Day and night
Night and day
Wiping away spots
That were not there

It was his only way
PTSD
To keep away
The silent demons

Vexing and oppressing
The military veteran
In his soul
In his mind

Thousands on thousands
Maybe millions or even billions
Military men
Washing and waxing

Their vehicles every day

JUNE 24 2022

ROE VS WADE OVERTURNED…TO LITTLE TO LATE WHO GIVES A DAMN? You got women walking around every day all day saying to men come and get it with the way they feature themselves and the way they dress and now all of a sudden the government wants to try to wash his hands of the abortion calamity when the horse is already out of the barn, why not just make sex illegal? l and then there would not have to be any rulings like this.. Female liberation so called. Love American style.

THE NEGRO HAS AN INHERITANCE

my name is yaiquab yisrael. And this is the Israelite sons flight radio program that I love to do every Wednesday and Friday at 8pm Pacific Standard Time. I want to begin by giving thanks to my Heavenly Father my earthly mother for this incredible opportunity to take my life my energies, my mental, spiritual and physical energies to be a light for the God of Abraham, Isaac, and Jacob. I am a fisher of men and this is my ministry. I have a website twelve tribes israelites.com all lowercase lettering spelled together. I have a room on Facebook called the upper row where I invite likeminded sons and daughters to join me for the sake of ministry, and to help you walk by faith and not by sight, by Scripture posting from different books every day to help you to bear fruit, while we are in this reality.

Now I also write books where if you type in my name yaiquab yisrael and you go to Amazon and type in my name, my books should come up. Now I am a brother who only fully believes in Redeeming the time. And my give is to minister and try to help other Hebrew Israelite sons and daughters of light, to aspire to do ministry with whatever light that you have. That is the purpose for my room, on Facebook and in addition, I am trying to start a nationwide ministry where I can call on brethren throughout the United States in case the call for charity goes out. For a brother or sister who lives in your area, I simply want to be a point of contact to especially sisters with children when the call goes out, just send me your email and the city you live in and I can direct you. If I get a request for charity. Then I can alert you to someone in your area that you can minister to.

Now I named the title of the program tonight. negros sons of light and daughters of light when I say sons of light, I mean that androgynously both sons and daughters. The Negro sons of light have an inheritance the 12 tribes of Israel we have an inheritance. Now, the things that the whole world wishes to have we have, if you read the Scripture, it says that, for our sakes, our Heavenly Father has created the world, now I believe that's in the book of Enoch. The 12 tribes of Israel, you negros, Latinos, and Native Americans, we have an inheritance.

Now, on my radio programs, I always like to talk about relationships. I love to use the analogy of relationships. Because the same principle applies in the worship of the Father. A lot of the answers that apply spiritually run off of the same principle as earthly relationships. Messiah asked Peter, Peter, do you love me? And he replied, yes, Lord you know, I do. And he said, feed my sheep. I mentioned that because Messiah asked Peter, do you love me? The same thing is said in the world, between a man and woman but in this day and age, it could be a man and a man. But the point is the worship of the Father. It needs to be more than head knowledge. There needs to be a spiritual inclination to put the world away and do things that are pleasing. To the father, because of sincerity, and not necessarily because of reward, we live in a society that only looks to compensation for what they have done. No One Out gives the Heavenly Father.

I want to digress for a second because another thing I like to do on my radio programs is testify. Recently I testified of being able to minister to a couple of sisters. And a couple of days later, after the Spirit moved me to look at a vehicle that I wanted. I would say it was a day later I was sitting in that vehicle. It was mine. I also want to testify of something you wouldn't think I will testify about. The Heavenly Father blesses us in many ways. I'm sure you know not always materially speaking. Now this just happened yesterday. I went for a drive. I hung out for a couple of hours. I went to get something to eat. And I would say I came back maybe three or four hours later. Don't you know that When I got back into my apartment, I had left the stove on high, but the pot which had only a little bit of food in it did not catch fire. brethren and sisters, please let me repeat, the stove I have I turned it up on high and forgot about it. I had a pot on the stove. The eye of the stove and I forgot about it. Brethren it should have burned the apartment down and when I came back into the apartment, I could immediately smell that something was burning. I went to the stove and simply turned it off realizing that it had been on for three or four hours but did not burn my apartment down.

The stove was on high, blessings are not always what we think they are. There are blessings of protection, blessings of wisdom, blessings of safety that every day shows that Heavenly Father and the angels surrounding you and protecting you. We don't know how many times we have been ministered to by the angels sent from the Heavenly Father.

And let me digress for a second. Did anyone see big Judas video on the angels, their names, their hours of the week and days we should make prayer and supplication to them? You ought to check out that video that the brother put out. To me is proof that we are on the very doorstep because every day we are being more and more enlightened. How to approach the Heavenly Father.

 the Heavenly Father has a solution for the witness of the world. What I mean is for the abortion of the world. The Heavenly Father has a solution for the corruption in government that we are currently under. Heavenly Father has a solution for the injustice for the murdering for the vexation and oppression and affliction of the 12 tribes Hebrew Israelites the Heavenly Father has a perfect solution. You want to know what it is called? It's called World War Three... World War Three is the perfect solution for the way the world has held the children of Israel in bondage and captivity. World War Three is the solution. And then the world will realize his punishment is just because we oppressed the children of Israel all these years World War Three. Did anyone seen a video where a Russian official responded to something a British Army General said about engaging Russia in battle? Now the actual words of this Russian General were that if Britain thought to engage Russia, then Britain will cease to exist...will cease to exist... that is the situation going on right now. In Europe, that most likely, we do not pay attention to, we hear lies in our main stream media telling us that Ukraine is winning the war and overcoming the Russian invasion. But the situation is such that now they are even having to admit that they are losing the war going on right now with Russia.

Russia every day is constantly gaining ground. Now again, the things that I am talking about so far as the hostilities going on over there is because this is not something a brother or sister would normally bring to your attention when talking about spiritual things. I bring it up because I know that the Scriptures speak of the day of the Lord. It speaks of a year of wrath. It speaks of the Israelites not being appointed to wrath. So, the closer we come to hostilities, beginning sons and daughters of light cannot be here.

This is good news brethren. The world was created for the Hebrew Israelites. Brethren, we have an incredible inheritance. When you look at TV, make sure you look for the programs along the lines of "The Secret Life of billionaires" and the fantastic dainties of life that they enjoy.

Brethren that is talking about you. You are the billionaires of this current reality you own all the gold; you own all the silver. Have you not heard of First Peter?

"Peter, an apostle of Messiah to the strangers scattered throughout, Pontus, Galatia cappa dosha Asia and Bithynia, elect according to the Fore knowledge of God the Father through sanctification of the Spirit unto obedience and sprinkling of the blood of Jesus Christ. Grace until you and peace be multiplied. Blessed be the Father and God of our Lord Jesus Christ, which according to his abundant mercy, the hath begotten us again unto a lively hope by the resurrection of Jesus Christ from the dead, to an inheritance, incorruptible, and undefiled that fade if not away. reserved in heaven, for you, who are kept by the power of God through faith unto salvation. ready to be revealed in the last time, wherein you greatly rejoice through now for a season if need be ye are in heaviness, through manifold temptations, that the trial of your faith being much more precious than of gold that perishes, though and be tried with fire might be found and to praise and honor and glory at the appearing of Messiah".

Brethren the Negro has an inheritance. The Latino on their father's side has an inheritance the Native American as an inheritance, that inheritance is Psalm 37 4 "Delight thyself also in the Lord. And He shall give me the desires of thine heart". Brethren, we have an inheritance. And when you look at this reality two thirds of our nation love this present reality. It only gets worse. For the oppressor nations from here on out, but it gets better every day. For you Hebrew Israelites. You know that the days are number the "X" across America is only a few months away. It is unmistakably, the work of the Heavenly Father, showing the world the judgment to come. Has anyone heard of the situation in kalingrad? a region, a territory of Russia tucked in between Poland and Lithuania? Has anyone heard of the situation over there? It is a small enclave that belongs to Russia. But it is surrounded by the European Union. And just recently Lithuania said we are going to cut off nearly a majority of the cargo that goes to Kalingrad. Russia has stated you will pay a price if you do not allow our goods to go through. Lithuania is a part of the European Union and they are really doing what the United States is telling them to do.

Brethren, I save this to point out the perilous times we are in. Does anyone know that the Ukraine is now being considered to join the European Union? Does anyone know what that means? It Is the United States looking for a reason to join this conflict. Because we know the jig is up. And we must find a way to engage Russia because we are broke. Nobody wants the dollar because it's not backed by anything. And nations are turning to gold backed currency. Brethren Matthew 24 is unfolding right before our eyes, did anyone see the article where an artificial intelligence robot hired a lawyer to prove it was alive? brethren these things are really, really happening. The current argument about abortion is another big distraction while the secret agendas go on for depopulation, for world domination and to erase the memory of the God of Abraham, Isaac, and Jacob that part of the agenda has been accomplished.

The God of Abraham, Isaac and Jacob has been forgotten about, brethren, Messiah said his spirit shall not always strive with man. This is the time to work on your testimony. To work for the treasure in heaven that faded not away reserved for you sons and daughters of light. We have come to the end of all our timelines that we know about. If you know about the depopulation agenda spoken of in the Book of Mormon, chapter 43. And if you know about the Georgia Guidestones and operation lockstep and agenda 2030 and agenda 21 and prophecies like the st Malachi prophecy about this Pope being the last pope and Revelation chapter six, verse three and the blood moons in Psalm 83 Deuteronomy 28 It lets you know we have come to the point.

I want to give thanks to my heavenly father or mother for this incredible opportunity.

Join me Wednesday and Friday 8pm Pacific Standard Time. And until I see you again may peace be unto you

shalom

I like you Vlad

I like you Vlad
Never met you
but I sure like you

Anytime
Anywhere
There is someone
Who knows what is right,

And fair

Then more power to you
You are my kind
A Libra as well
Like me

You make me proud
Because I know
What a Libra believes
Truth and justice

For real

The brotherhood of man
Devoid of evil
I like you Vlad
I know you have faults

And made mistakes

Haven't we all?

Sometimes
When the call comes
From on high
Certain qualities
Are needed

To walk alone
To have strong character
Fiery passion
Love of what's right

I like you Vlad
You know in your heart
The reason for those bio labs

In Ukraine

Only a few feet away
From your border

For eight years
The people cried out
In Donbass and Luguentz
Both day and night

They cried out
The bombs
They fall
No relief in sight

The Ukrainians
All because
Our language

And culture
They despise
We know
What hatred is

It is called
The azov battalion
It is called
Victoria Nuland

It is called
Neoconservative
It is called
The Pentagon

It is called
American funded
Bio labs
To seek and search for

Depopulation
Of the Slavic
Of the Donbass
Of the luganz

Of the Russian kind

I like you Vlad
Highly criticized
It does not matter

The truth is never popular

And very few
To lift its banner
I like you Vlad
History will too

A vibration

Life is
A vibration
Dwelling in each of us
From which

We cannot
Turn away from
Embedded in the soul
We March each day

To a steady beat
Not heard
Only felt
Cosmically

Even this
Greatly glorifies
The father
Who art in heaven

Life and vibrations
It has to be this way
For better or worse
It's mystery very great

Life is vibration
Even when we leave
For new dimensions
A new reality

Of light
And sound
In color
And white gowns

Where new vibrations
Never before seen
Await each one of us
In the heavenlies

Based on
Faith and works
And deeds
Of love and sharing

The choice is ours

Which vibration
We come under
This is the way

It has to be

July 2022

Today was one of days where I found myself ruminating on the blessing and vexation of being elected to have faith in God. Why I torture myself engaging in this behavior from time to time is beyond me. I count this type of mind to the human experience but still, It is a practice I'd rather not. Engage in regularly for the most part. It's just that I cannot help it. It is a constant vexation to me. When I consider the daily grind of day to day. Same ol thing people going about day to day just surviving. In my heart I know that this is not living, its just trying to keep up an existence that we all know must come to a conclusion at some point. It is this type of thinking that has driven me to know about the unseen and it makes me wonder why the world I live in does not seem to feel the same way or maybe people do feel the way I feel but it's just so hidden in the psyche and never dealt with outwardly. In this reality people are willing to work 30 40 years to live for five to 10 years after their career is over for little peace and what they feel is security. I have never really understood this type of thing. But I guess in this reality there is just no other way to exist. For me I cannot live this way I must live work and have faith in whatever is eternal. I've never been willing to exert all my energy for that which is only temporary. And 100 years of living on earth to me is temporary. I thank the god of Abraham Isaac and Jacob to not just live for the earthly Earthly but to live for the eternal. In my mind this is the greatest gift imaginable and oftentimes I do not understand the grace behind it, but I certainly do receive it with Thanksgiving. I don't know what I would do with myself if I did not have something on a day to day basis to chew on mentally and consider and tie myself in knots at the same time. What an enigma I am

No wisdom in teman

Thank you for joining me my name is yaiquab yisrael and this is the Israelite sons of light radio program, a ministry that I have for your benefit for you Hebrew Israelite, sons of light and daughters of light. I have a room on Facebook called the upper room and a website. If the things I say resonate with you, where you can go and get in contact with me for ministry and information. I want to also say that I am an author and I have written books where if you go to Amazon you can type in my name and my books should come up. I write books basically they are diary in form and I try to write from a Hebrew Israelite perspective. So, you can go there and check it out. There's an option to look inside to see what type of things I like to try to write about. And I firmly believe that if I am a brother who can write books, then so can you, basically all you're doing is just basically speaking, as you were to a friend about different things, your perspective.

Okay, now, the name of the program tonight. "Is there no more wisdom in teman"? No more wisdom and Teman spoken up in Jeremiah chapter 49. No more wisdom in Teman. Now, I have a simple message for my nation, the Hebrew Israelites. My ministry is to proclaim there is another reality coming it belongs to the children of Israel, the Negro, the Latino, and Native American on their father's side. This kingdom is called the kingdom of God of Abraham, of Isaac and Jacob. And you are certainly invited you Hebrew Israelites to be a part of it. The invitation is hereby extended to you to prepare for it by way of faith and works and holiness and righteousness. Now I want to say I'm a brother that believes wholeheartedly that our nation is filled with brothers and sisters who have beautiful gifts. One way or another, as it says in Ephesians, I believe it is Ephesians where it talks about different ministrations of the spirit. Meaning we have different brethren in our nation right now. That can minister to you one way or another, to attract whatever your spirit gravitates to.

Basically, my ministry is an evangelical type ministry where my message is that I am a fisher of men. I seek to find brethren who wish to gravitate to do ministry, to join me in my room on Facebook and to help you to evolve to give you a foundation through the posting of scripture from various books that are meant to help you build a foundation and to give you the confidence to engage in what type of ministry you desire, wherever the Spirit leads you. My message is to whatever you do, Redeem the time. One way or another.

If you have a gift of serving by way good deeds, maybe you have the gift of being able to deal with small groups of brethren to speak to them, or to minister some type of way, or whether you are elected to speak to many brethren. You know, best what is in your spirit to be the best light that you can be for our nation, especially at this time since we are approaching the end of our captivity, and our restoration as the 12 tribes of Israel. Now, I wanted to speak tonight on the situation going on the confluence of events that clearly point to the fact that revelation and other verses are clearly showing the end of our captivity to the oppressor nations. Now, it is the agenda of the oppressor nations to conceal the identity of the 12 tribes, which up until now has worked marvelously. Mainly through Christianity, and Catholicism. We are witnessing in the world today. The first rain drops of divine judgment coming upon our oppressors for the treatment of the 12 tribes of Israel. Now, when you read the Scripture, the heavenly Father, he has different modes of how he exercises judgment. He shows us in the Book of Judges the example of the Canaanite woman who struck down an Israelite because he had a foreign wife in Judges chapter 15. Giving you the example of the heavenly Father can use even someone of another nation to bring judgment, on the oppressor nation. Or, as it says in Ezekiel chapter 25. He can and he will use the children of Israel to exercise vengeance. Which is really interesting because in both cases, the Heavenly Father uses a method to bring judgment. He says that Vengeance is mine. I will repay the oppressor nations do not realize this, they do not realize the children of Israel or else they would not have done the things historically that they have done to us. So, in concealing our identity, they have sealed their judgment.

When you look at the news information, outlets you see the only thing the oppressor nations can do is talk about gold and silver to save them and how you have to store up and buy gold and silver. Even though you have no money. You have to acquire gold and silver or they will talk about politics is their only Savior and how only politics can save them. The news outlets are pretty much 24-hour political discussion and trying to find a solution politically to the different social and economic and geopolitical situations going on in the world today. They talk about guns. They talk about the different governmental parties, the

Republicans and the Democrats and how they have to move them out of office. And then Donald Trump will save them. They do all these things in order to try to save their current blessing of rulership of the world.

They speak of surviving. They speak of how they need to explore Mars so that they can start all over again and implement a great reset. They do not speak of repentance. They speak of anything other than giving glory to the God of Abraham, Isaac, and Jacob for all these things that are coming upon them, showing the world that the Heavenly Father is able to implement his will over the oppressors of the children of Israel and the blasphemers of His Word, divine judgment and part of this judgment that we see is there is no more wisdom in Teman. In other words, the American Edomite governmental ruling system, there is no more wisdom to prosper, to evolve except it be for their own demise.

Reading from Jeremiah, chapter 49. It says, Therefore, behold, the days come, saith the Lord that I will cause an alarm of war to be heard in Raba of the Ammonites. Now I think this is talking about the Middle East area and it shall be a desolate heap. And her daughter shall be burned with fire then shall Israel be heir unto them, that were his heirs. The restoration of the 12 tribes is what he's saying there. Howl heshbon, AI is spoil. Cry the daughters of Raba gird you with sackcloth, lament and run to and fro by the hedges, for they shall go into captivity. And his priests and his princes together. Now, let me stop there in verse three of Jeremiah 49 and say this. I believe it is speaking of those who have had us in captivity and have oppressed us. As far as I know heshbon and AI were ancient cities of modern-day Jordan who at one point our oppressors, the Hebrew Israelites and I believe that this can also be applied to Esau and his religious, Catholic Christian, entities that have oppressed the 12 tribes of Israel, verse four, wherefore glorious thou in the valleys by flowing Valley, backsliding daughter, that trusted in her treasures, saying who shall come unto me? In my opinion, this is speaking of America, who trust in her high position and she glories and being over the valleys, in other words, having a position of advantage to defend against the enemies of her nation of her rulership because of her high position. Behold, I will bring a fear upon thee saith the Lord God of hosts, from all those that be about the you shall be driven out every man right forth, none shall gather up him that wonder. Now if you are watching the news, you should be able to see that there are a group of nations called the BRICS nations, Brazil, Russia, India, China and

South Africa, which are creating their own currency and their own trading bloc's trading within each other's borders, and other nations are joining them. The United States is not included neither or European Union countries. This is because there is no more wisdom in teaming. The rulership of this country of America has no ability to escape the situations that are going on that are leaving the United States and the European Union to certain nuclear war. The current situation is orchestrated by the God of Abraham, Isaac, and Jacob to where Europe and Russia and China Europe and the United States must go to war with one another. There is no more wisdom in teman, which I am using teman as a prototype of America to politically solve the current situation. The Heavenly Father has not granted them the ability to find a way of peace. With Russia, the truth has condemned America the biological laboratories in the Ukraine and the corruption that we have been behind for the last eight years, installing Perl, Western governments. And now the chickens have come home to roost Russia found out about the biological laboratories and their purpose. The United States knows that. Russia has found out all that is left for us. To do meaning America is to lie about it. And to tell the world that it is a lie. But it is a lie that this country is telling to the face of the God of Abraham, Isaac and Jacob. And now, the heavenly Father, in conjunction with all the other signs is clearly blowing a long trumpet to tell the children of Israel it is time to prepare to come home.

A storm is coming. It will not turn back. Verse 10, Jeremiah 49 But I have made Esau bare. I have uncovered his secret places and he shall not be able to hide himself. His seed is spoiled and his neighbors and he is not, meaning no more. I want to speak a word to you younger Israelites. It is a very perilous time for you younger Hebrew Israelites because the pull of the world on your soul on your spirit is very strong.

The older Hebrew Israelites have seen the spirit of our oppressors. We have seen the evolving of times past until now and how things have gotten to this point. But you younger Israelites you still have a spirit within you that wants to see the world and wants to take part of the dainties of the world of America of this life. And although it may not seem like it, Revelation 18 proclaims the destruction of America in one hour and her dainties being removed being, the fast food, the shiny cars, the high paying job, these are things that with every new day are getting closer to its conclusion. And younger Hebrew Israelites must if you have any spiritual inclination, take advantage of it right now. By prayer by supplication by meditation by reading and studying. We are in a time where the warnings are very clear. Two thirds of our nation is in danger and that includes young Israelites.

I pray that you search and examine your soul and draw near to the God of Abraham, Isaac and Jacob. Look around you, look at what's going on economically which is probably the biggest indicator that this reality has come to a close. Revelation chapter six, verse three and up is more evident than anything. Not to mention the return of the planet Pluto to finish its cycle which ends in judgment in 2024. The end of the timelines as we have known them. The Book of Mormon speaks of an overflowing scourge in chapter 43. That most certainly seems to indicate the current virus. Matthew chapter 24 is obviously being played out. There is an "x" that will form across America in 2024 For now, all these are part of a blowing trumpet. Which brings to mind there was a president whose last name is Trump and the vice president's last name was pence. This is absolutely beyond the realm of coincidence. It is the finger of God. The nations know that it is but it is too late for them to make amends for the evil that has been done to the Hebrew Israelites.

Russia is a time clock they will soon overrun Ukraine. The United States no we must go to war because of the certain demise of the dollar and their inability to trade with other nations. They must go to war. And with each new day, they are getting closer and closer to overthrowing the Ukrainian government, which has been a hub of corruption for money laundering and human trafficking and it has been America that has been behind this corruption. Brethren, if anything I say resonates with you. I pray that you would contact me on my website twelvetribesisraelites.com all spelled together lowercase lettering or contact me on Facebook and join me and my other brethren. And let me try to build you up to encourage you to endure in the faith and to write your testimony while you are in the earth, that's all that life is for. To write your testimony while you are in the earth. Let it be filled with thanksgiving with study and prayer and being the best light that you can be helping other Hebrew Israelites to draw near to the God of Abraham, Isaac and Jacob now

until I see you again
Wednesday or Friday 8pm Pacific Standard Time.

the parasite and leech

one sucks blood
the other sucks people
A Leech
Sucks blood

A Leech
Can be
A positive thing
When the blood

Infected

A parasite
Sucks people
Of their life
And resources

And never repays
What they took

One is a bug
The other is a person

A Leech
Can help someone
A parasite
Destroys

It all depends
On how you look at it
One can help
The other can kill

I knew a man
A parasite
Of a man
Always taking

And giving nothing
In return
Except grief
And sorrow

A parasite
Of a man
A Leech
In a negative way

Instead
of sucking your blood
he sucked
Your wallet away

Living off of you
Was all
He could do
A shame of a man

Hard to look at
Always looking
To Leech off someone
Because to him

It was easier
That way
Blaming others
For his own sins

A Leech of a man
In a negative way
Hopelessly lost
To the beast Kingdom

With other parasites
Day by day

Draining resources
From the human race

No good to themselves
Except their flesh

Their carnal self
Devoid of spirit
And dignity
Daily begging

And addiction riddled
A parasite of a man

A Leech if you will
Sucking the life
Out of any
Living thing

No good to anyone
Or himself

Far distant
From the eternal Kingdom
From the knowledge of
From the power of

The God of Abraham
The God of Isaac
The God of Jacob

retribution

Now do you see?
Now do you see why?
We call you the devil?
You evil demon

White people in power
Never satisfied
Unless destruction
And blood murder

You leave behind

And now you've done it
You've really done it now
Provoking and pushing
The Russian bear

Only one problem
Now he's fighting back
And he is in the right
And so, win he must

Against your evil demon
Bloodthirsty lust
For things that are not yours
But a price you will pay

Painful it will be

You demon white people
The ones in power
You political ruling elite
You've done it now

Starting with Barack Obama
That famous white devil
2014
The maidan revolution

That white devil
Barack Obama
Masquerading
as a negro

funding biolabs
In the Ukraine
To create
A virus to depopulate

Using another white devil
The Ukraine
Ukraine the white devil
Bombing and bleeding
Its own people

With the help of
The United States
Of white people
With arms and weapons

And billions of dollars

Because the white devil knew
His time had come
So, it was all or nothing
ZERO sum

And NATO
Another white devil
After all these years
How come you never learned

After all the wars
Done on your soil
You mean to tell me
You want one more?

So, you will have it

Your wish will come true
When you are
Blown to hell and back

With your boyfriend
The United States
Of white people
All at once

And once for all
When Russia and China
Bombs began to fall
On your evil corruption

Your demonic devil dealing
And you're lying and deceit
Through the Jewish owned media
Amazing when you think about it

You actually believe
All this evil
You will get away
You have no clue

You are writing
Your own death certificate
All your crimes listed
In great detail

The judge
The God of Abraham
Of Isaac
And Jacob

All this
For the evil committed
Against the children of Israel
These past thousands of years

For the stealing of our identity

And labor
And the endless shooting
Of our nation

You evil demon devil dog
White man power structure
Taking communion
Passing laws

Despising God
United States
Of white people

Little canoe

I was afraid
To admit it
But like a man
At the end of his retirement

Sweetly slowly
Drifting and rolling
Inhaling roses
Of the past

Closing in
On that final day
Looking back
Giving thanks

That's me
No more time
For life change
All lessons

Fully learned
The passions of youth
The fire that burned
For a season

Now
In my wake

The lose seasons of life
That tugged at my soul
The fires of emotions
Wild thoughts and mistakes

All in my wake

I was on a canoe
Drifting very slowly
My feet

Over this side hanging

The raging white waters
Behind me
Called life
But I overcame them

Now I float
On a bubbly brewing lake
Towards my final destination
Eternal rest and glory

The fires of life
Greatly subsided
Now I float
On a canoe

On the lake of life
Tall glass
Sweet lemonade
By my side

I sit
I reminisce
About the times
Whether I would make it

The confusion
The chaos
The world telling me this
Telling me that
Do it this way

Never the right answer
Making it worse
When you were young
And truly sincere

Looking for
The right road

On which your canoe
To steer

But I heard
Someone say
It is within you
It is called

The Kingdom way

And I was glad
So, in my canoe
My journey began
All the way

To this point
Finish line ahead
Long glass of lemonade
In my hand

No moment wasted
Every second taste
To build my soul
This quiet Oasis

And I was glad

this is the Israelite, sons of light radio program that I tried to do every Wednesday and Friday at 8pm Pacific Standard Time. Last week I was sick, so I did not get a chance to do a Friday program. But I want to give thanks to my Heavenly Father and earthly mother, that I am feeling better and here I am back again. I want to say that I am a fisher of men. I write books. I have this ministry and a ministry on Facebook called the upper room where you are invited to join me and my other brethren so that I can do my best to try to minister to you sons and daughters of like to help you hopefully, to aspire to want to do ministry or if you need to be encouraged on a daily basis. I can try to help with that as well.

I am a brother who has prayed to be in this position where I can try to dedicate myself to being a light pointing to the God of Abraham, Isaac and Jacob which I consider to be my only reason for my reality. I do not say that I do these things perfectly. But that should be even more encouragement for you to receive the word and to put your own flavor on it. All of us have different vibrations that we are under and different abilities. To bring out the over standing as best we can. According to what we know. None of us has anything that we did not receive. So, all the glory but must go to the God of Abraham, Isaac, and Jacob. You will find that my radio programs I constantly refer to the God of Abraham, Isaac and Jacob, the God of the Scriptures, the God of the 12 tribes of Israel you negros Latinos and Native Americans.

I am an author. I write books you can type in my name on Amazon Yaiquab Yisrael and my books should come up. Book writing is an activity I highly recommend for anyone under the sound of my voice. The technology in the current reality makes it simple as simple can be in order to write a book. It is the equivalent of simply talking to a friend over the phone and letting the computer do all the work for you.

Now, the last couple of weeks I've been sharing that I want to establish a nationwide network of brethren to join hands with me to minister to brethren throughout our nation who have come upon hard times. And are in need of being ministered to Food wise. I would like anyone under the sound of my voice to contact me if you know of someone in your area. And I will let the nation know of the brother or sister and hopefully it will be able to reach the ears of a nearby brother or sister who can do ministry for the requesting brother or sister.

I especially am trying to target sisters with children. Okay Having said all that the title of my program tonight is Russia is a time clock. Russia is a time clock. Now let me say this. If you are like me a Gnostic Hebrew, Israelite son of light and you subscribe to the Nag Hammadi. It is a book a part of the Dead Sea Scrolls and it has many books within it. And when you read it, it speaks of three different spiritual realms. It speaks of a hylic realm a pneumatic realm and a material realm. Now these represent sons and daughters of light as the pneumatic spiritual sons and daughters of light and then you have the hylic realm. And this represents brethren who are less than fully committed to the light and over standing of the spiritual word. And you have the material realm, and this makes up the spirits in the world who have no spiritual inclination and are given to the carnal senses and the influences of the here and the now.

Now when you read about the three spiritual realms, you quickly should realize that we are in a reality that is by far the majority. The material realm, otherwise known as the beast kingdom and that alone makes you want to leave the current reality because it is a godless reality. The light shineth in the darkness, but the darkness comprehended it not, and you brethren of the hylic realm are greatly surrounded. Every day you must overcome the material realm in drawing nearer to the God of Abraham, Isaac and Jacob, it is highly important that you learn how to swing that sword meaning the Word of God, because sometimes you have to and there were even times where I had to lay a curse on someone and I can testify the things that I have had to proclaim on someone have come to pass, and I am not ashamed to confess this thing, because I know it probably makes me sound like a witch for which I do not really care. The Scriptures speak of binding and loosing a spirit. Now, I bring this up especially for you sisters because we are approaching a very dangerous, perilous time and some of you sisters may be on your own. It seems like the present time in our nation there is great over standing going on. About the angels I have been seeing many videos about the angels and Arc angels.

I seem to recall when I was younger, how women knew these things. Spiritual things. The angels it seems the women I observed in my younger years, automatically knew to call on the angels for help and now the overstanding is much greater and detailed. Now, I want to say what I'm about to say for the sake of the sisters in our nation. And personally, I really believe the majority of you already know these things. It seems that in our nation our women had to rely on the angels in order to raise our families. They had to turn to a greater power in order to raise our families in the earlier days. Praying for food, praying for protection, praying for healing and using natural remedies I've seen to recall the female principal doing these things automatically. It is part of the female principal miracle and how they have been gifted and equipped supernaturally to endure and survive in the male principal world. And so, I want to say again, we are approaching a time where Revelation Chapter Six is on the increase. It is in my spirit to look diligently around the world. On video on anything I can get my hands on information wise, so that I may run and tell my own nation and what I have been seeing is the approach of perilous times. especially prophesied for the latter half of this year. And you sisters with children are going to have to learn to take advantage of the different angels and the hours of their ministry. And how to pray and make supplication to them. This is something the current kingdom and reality will not teach us. They never could. They never will. Now as I was saying the title of this radio program tonight is Russia is a time clock. One of the strongest indicators for me to know how near we are to the restoring of ourselves. Meaning you sons and daughters of light, brothers and sisters of faith is to look at what is going on in the Ukraine. I want to report to you Russia will take over that whole country. It is only a matter of time if the Ukraine and the European Union and NATO do not find a way to reach a peace settlement. Ukraine will fall to Russia. Actually, it already is a part of Russia. The only thing basically that separates the Ukraine from Russia are cultural differences. But the European Union they need the Ukraine so that they can have Bio Labs and a means to station military assets right there on Russia's border. It is not working. Russia is cutting off the natural gas of which they supply to Europe in bulk especially to Germany and Italy. The winter months are only a couple of months away. And if the situation does not change, there will be a disaster.

Russia is a time clock. Something has to give. They are forming their own trading bloc, Russia and China with other Eastern Asian countries leaving out Europe and the United States which should tell you brethren, anyone looking for Messiah. We are in a death struggle right now. I did not even mention 2024 and the X across America I did not even mention the top of the Pope retiring and nominating a so- called Black Pope and the st Malachy Prophecy, predicting the current would be the last one.

I think everyone knows about the current spread of the virus and the secret agenda so far as that is concerned. These are all time clocks. They are ticking to a conclusion. Russia is a time clock warning that a conclusion an explosion must come to pass imminently. There are many time clocks that are ticking down right at this very moment. The present administration is a time clock. It is coming out more and more about the corruption of the White House. It is pretty much common knowledge that the current administration was elected fraudulently when the fall approaches the midterm elections, and the Democrats are removed from office. Then the Republicans will begin investigations when they take power. The truth will come out and the current administration will be exposed. It could cause a civil uprising. The lights we have never seen before. When people see the truth about the fraud that they were tricked on, the situation is a time clock. The midterm elections are a time clock.

 Europe is a time clock because they need oil and gas the refinery in the south in Louisiana that America was supplying Europe with oil and gas recently suffered an accident disabling the ability of America to ship gas and oil to help buffer against the cut off that Russia read recently implemented against Europe. Algeria and Libya also recently for some reason or another, greatly reduced or stopped shipping, oil and gas to Europe. Europe is a time clock. They cannot go on without oil and gas supplies. The truth is a time clock and it must come out the powers that be know they are corrupt and they are simply try to hold on to the rulership of the earth but they are out of options. The last option available to the elite of the Western Hemisphere is to go to war with Russia because war is profit. But when the truth gets out, people will rise up and America will fall under its own weight . This is the God of Abraham, Isaac, and Jacob fighting for the 12 tribes. I recently read an article or heard news account of the brother in Ohio gun down and the nations of the world never learn when one of us is murder. 100 of them is murdered.

 Brethren join me in my room on Facebook called the Upper Room. Send me a friend invite. Let's Redeem the time as we watch the oppressor nations come to their conclusion.

Join me Wednesday Friday 8pm Pacific Standard Time

.i want to give thanks to my heavenly father earthly mother,

 until I see you again peace be unto you

Shalom

Hear the word of the lord

this is the Israelite sons of flight radio program which I try to do every Wednesday and Friday 8pm Pacific Standard Time. I want to give thanks to my Heavenly Father earthly mother for this incredible opportunity to be a light while I am in this reality, to testify of God of Abraham, Isaac and Jacob and to seek out other like minded brethren for the purpose of ministry, in my room on Facebook, where I try to encourage brethren to evolve to ministry, or if you just need daily encouragement from the Scripture, I try to provide that as well.

I am a fisher of men. And I have this ministry, for the purpose of fulfilling the words of Messiah to seek and save that which is lost. And to feed my sheep. I have a website. If anything I say resonates with you, where if you want you can get in contact with me it is called twelvetribesisraelites.com all lowercase lettering and spelled out twelvetribesisraelites.com.

Okay, I named the title of the program tonight. "Here the word of the Lord". Now, before I begin, allow me to digress for a second I'm sure many of you have probably heard of the brother. That was shot 60 times, fleeing a traffic stop. But did you know the white man who's shot at those people on July 4, killing six people and injuring 20 was also stopped at a traffic stop and attempted to flee. And do you know they took him alive? It is just another indicator of the deep seated hatred of the oppressor nations against us, the same circumstance minus the shooting and the brother ended up dead and by this time if you are over the age of 40 you are pretty much numb to these things happening to us.

To me, one of the strongest instigators of the people of God the 12 tribes, the children of Israel, Negro Latino and Native Americans on your father's side. It is just another strong indicator of who we are. The things that we endure in this present reality. We are now in a situation where the agenda of the gods of this world have worked completely to erase the memory of the God of Abraham Isaac and Jacob to erase the memory of the 12 tribes of Israel by providing various events of all kinds to take away our focus on who we are and trying to draw near to the God of Abraham, Isaac, and Jacob and to be a light to our own nation. The agenda of the gods of this world seems to realize the kingdom of the powers that be, has come to its conclusion. The testimonies of the reappearance of Pluto concluding its cycle in 2024 for the testimony of the X across America in 2024. The end of the Hebrew timelines as we know them, and presently, in our day and age the current influenza meant to depopulate is in full effect. And did you know that just recently, even the European Union confessed that the needle jab damages the immune system.

Now having said that, I might as well say this. I will probably get a strike for even saying that. You're going to have to catch my videos on bitchute. I have a link in the description box that you should be able to catch up on my latest videos. In case you come on my channel and I am not there for however long. Sometimes I cannot do videos because lately I have been sick a lot.

Now I want to say this also that I forgot to say I want to have a nationwide ministry where if anyone, primarily of our nation especially sisters with children who have food shortage needs to contact me or if anyone under the sound of my voice knows of anyone to contact me so I can share the information on my programs per chance a brother or sister lives nearby and can do ministry to the brother or sister in me. Love covering a multitude of sins. So please anyone who knows of anyone that needs to be ministered to let me know and I will announce the information in hopes that someone will hear.

 The title of the program is "Hear the Word of the Lord". Hear the Word of the Lord. One difference between an Israelite who hears meaning it affects their actions. And an Israelite who does not hear because their actions are not affected. The difference is the brother who hears has an anointing on him. He realizes the word is anointed. There is a magic to the Word of God. That is not easily explained. We live in a world where the current reality loves to get off on the life of other people. Taking the focus away from ourself. In other words, to live vicariously it is one of the great evils but if you are elected and anointed, the word of God is magic to your ears. When you read the anointed word, all types of over standing should flood your mind. The danger is when you hear and then you forget the person that you looked at in the mirror. We all know what the will of Messiah is, to take the word of God and do something with it. And other words to return his word with interest. That is the purpose of the word we read and study. Now, I want to read the Word of the Lord because He is speaking to us about the current day and age. We are in reading from second esdras chapter 15. It says Behold, see, speak thou in the ears of my people. The words of prophecy, which I will put in thy mouth, saith the LORD and cause them to be written in paper. Four they are faithful and true. Fear not the imaginations against thee let not the incredulity of them trouble thee that speak against thee. Now, verse three is very interesting, because there are brethren in our nation who do ministry and in a sense, try to return the word of the Lord with interest. And so, the Heavenly Father encourages you brothers who are involved day by de actively seeking to be a light while you're in this reality. We don't all agree with one another. We may not like one another. But the important thing is to worship and sincererity and truth, verse four, for all the unfaithful shall die, in their unfaithfulness. Behold, saith the Lord. I will bring plagues upon the world. The sword famine death, and destruction. Now, you may say these things have always been here. I would agree with you but I would add that since 2019, there has been a marked increase in secret agendas met to produce a massive black horse as in the horse of revelation six, verse three in death, through means we have never, ever seen before. The Heavenly Father says Behold saith the Lord, I will bring plagues upon the world, the Sword famine, death and destruction we have the sword, wars and rumors of wars, famine. The prophecy of revelation six three a quart of wheat for a denarius, meaning a day's pay. Death and destruction. And you can imagine what that means… for wickedness half exceedingly polluted the whole earth and their hurtful works are fulfill you enlightened Hebrew Israelites. Do you see now why you should rejoice? As you look around, and you see the foundation of the oppressor nations cracking and you realize that we are the only people who have this hope of a better future of the Eternal Kingdom which the other oppressor nations desperately try to reason us out of. On a daily basis. It is a another play on the verse where Esau asked his father "has thou now only one blessing?". And even to this day, Esau is crying because he gave the birth right away. And there is nothing he can do to regain it. For wickedness have exceedingly polluted the whole earth and there are hurtful works are fulfilled.

Therefore, saith the Lord I will hold my tongue no more as touching their wickedness which they profanely commit neither will I suffer them in those things in which they wickedly exercise themselves. Behold the innocent and righteous blood cryeth unto me and the soles of the just complain continually and that is exactly the situation we are in today and not just the souls of the Israelites cry out to the God of Abraham, Isaac and Jacob. But there are the innocence of those who belong to the oppressor nations that cry out as well. It seems to me the gods of this world, realize they cannot have this present reality anymore. So therefore, no one can have it. If they cannot have it. Call to mine, the pigs and the man of the Gadarenes who cried out to Messiah Have you come to kill us before the time? meaning they know the time the powers that be the wicked that be they know the time of their demise.They know now is the time. A very interesting thing is in the land today. The people have no clue even in spite of the incredible information coming out, warning the whole world about the dangers of the big Vaccintion. You're going to have to figure out the word I want to use that I cannot eat even in a time when so much information is coming out about the injection and how it is meant to be a tool for reducing global population. Does anyone find it interesting that if you look at the time stamp of the moment, the first pillar of the Georgia Guidestones was knocked over. Do you realize the time was 333 on July 6 2022. Is that a coincidence? Or is that the elite telling us they know their time is over and they now have to speed up their agenda in order to take down as many people as they can while they still have time. Verse nine and therefore saith the Lord I will surely avenge them and receive unto me all the innocent blood from among them. He will avenge those who have initiated these agendas. For the purpose of depopulation. And He will avenge the Hebrew Israelites for the many 1000s of years that we have suffered at the hands of the oppressor nations. Hear ye the Word of the Lord. Behold, my people you 12 tribes Hebrew Israelites, Negro, Latino and Native American is led as a flock to the slaughter I will not suffer them now to dwell in the land of Egypt. But I will bring them with a mighty hand and stretched out arm and smite Egypt with plagues as before and will destroy all the land. Now if you were to ask me. I would not argue if you said that Egypt was America or is the world I believe a case can be made for both ideas. Egypt shall mourn and the foundation of it shall be smitten with the plague and punishment that God shall bring upon it. So here we have the Heavenly Father letting us know who is responsible for the things that are now coming on the earth. We know that he uses proxies to accomplish His will. They that tilled the ground shall mourn for their seeds shall fail through the blasting and hail and with a fearful constellation. Now, there are plenty of videos talking about crop failures and the conflagration in the Ukraine. Cutting roughly 30 Maybe even 40% of the world's grain production whoa to the world and them that dwell therein for the sword, and they're judgement draweth night and one people stand up to fight against another with swords and pains for their shall be sedition among men and invading one another. For they shall not regard their kings nor princes, in the course of their actions shall stand in their power I'm out of time.

Thank you for joining me

 I want to give thanks to the Heavenly Father earthly mother

Until I see you again,

peace be unto you. Shalom.

joe biden

I remember one time talking with my dad I asked him who he liked as president, he said Joe Biden, now this was before Joe Biden was even vice president. I cannot go on trying to write this book unless I write about my thoughts on this man. Joe Biden is quite amazing to me, he is a chameleon of a man he is not a leader, he is corrupt to the core, even his own family accuses him of being a pedophile, a man who has taken showers with his daughter a man who is the president of the United states and has a son on video consorting with prostitutes and engaging in drug use and yet here is a man who does not see any value in his dignity that he would step down because he is compromised and corrupt. Joe Biden is a man that tries to come across as an everyman but people who know… know, that he is a puppet of the Jews just like all American presidents. Joe Biden cares very little about personal dignity he cares about his own self-interest and this is embarrassing. I have come across information from the media detailing problems with his personal hygiene habits and how his advancing age prophecies that he most likely will not finish his term in office. And then our decline as a nation will increase exponentially with the vice president Karmala Harris. A woman whose political platform is simply that she is a woman of color. It seems to me that the God of Abraham Isaac and Jacob is saving her for dessert for America. I am convinced that she will be installed very soon when the Democratic Party finally comes to his senses and realizes they have a bumbling idiot for a president saying one thing and doing another and in between selling the nation's resources for personal self-dealing, and must do something now. Then they will be forced to install a cackling circular reasoning, callous, immoral woman who used sex for the purpose of advantage to ascend to the presidency. Me personally I will love it because America will get what it deserves. The fact that America absolutely has a blind spot for determining the character of its leaders means they get what they deserve. Every election cycle America has forgotten or has been put to sleep to the fact that its candidates do not give glory to the God of Abraham Isaac and Jacob they do not speak of biblical values and they do not have works to back it up or the knowledge to convince the skeptics of their sincerity of the truth of the word of God. We know potential candidates for political office will never ever take up the cause of the Hebrew Israelites 12 tribes so don't even ask. But still at least you would think a nation would be better at discerning the character based on history of an individual. But America is in no way astute at making those types of judgments when considering a leader, so America gets what it deserves and personally I love it.

The human experience at times can really be a trip there are some days actually a lot of days where I just feel flat out evil in my thinking and about people. I have the type of mind where I cannot understand why most people do not act like I believe they should in other words how is it? or why is it? that people act against their own best interests?. I believe what I am saying is choosing short term gain over long term consequences. In this day and age there is a strong proclivity to take the short money to sell out themselves or a nation for personal benefit, this thing vexes me to no end. I have simplified the issue in my mind, it is simply because there is No Fear of the God of Abraham Isaac and Jacob. It has become acceptable for people for governments for presidents and authorities to deceive and to cheat and to be immoral because it is accepted that there are no consequences. I count this as the greatest danger of all. As I consider the confluence of events which really are the judgments of the God of Abraham Isaac and Jacob I continually shake my head because these warnings are meant to warn people there is a God and he will judge and man is accountable to him although he may not think so now man will pay a price for his immorality for his withholding the truth in unrighteousness. Not to mention the total destruction of the children of Israel the Negro Latino,Native American on your fathers side. At the present I have noticed another grievous error in the Kingdom of man that previously I used to take note of but then put it in the back of my mind but now it has resurfaced again. What I am talking about is the rise of women leaders in the world ruling over men this is another thing that makes me shake my head it shows a clear disdain for the heavenly order of man as head of the woman and the Bible warning against violating that order it is a simple order it makes sense that the heavenly order prevents confusion. There is a fantastic rise in women leading men in this reality. I refuse to let it vex me like it did before because I do not care about this current reality because it does not fear the God of Abraham Isaac and Jacob and is lost in awaiting judgment a very painful judgment but still I watch with intrigue as the rise of women leading men with great intrigue. It is the mystery of iniquity it is the amazing prophecy of genesis chapter 3 coming to fruition where the desire of the woman shall be to her husband meaning her desire to rule over him. And this thing has come to pass it is a steady source of amazement to my mind. We are there we are there we have arrived at the point of no return everywhere in the world there is a tension that is palpable truly the world is a banjo string it is amazing to behold these things.

For me there are a couple of options except what I see in the media reports about the bank runs in China and the impending food shortages coming globally or to just shut the media off and out. The latter is an impossibility since I want to stay informed the best way that I can. I realized that in the United states there is a great deal of propaganda as I imagine there is in other countries in their media. But one way I know that the financial prices and the food shortage prices is true is because of what the scriptures tell me in revelation chapter 6. Even though I have been hearing of these things for a few months now it is hard for me to get over the power of the God of Abraham Isaac and Jacob to do what he prophesized he is going to do over the Kingdom of men. China is a very secretive society and they have implemented social mechanisms in order to control their people and their people comply they do not mind giving up their sovereignty even to the point of being locked inside their own apartments meaning locked inside as in their doors being welded shut. These are the type of things that I cannot get my mind around. The real issue in China is not the health of the people the real issue is the fact that they are bankrupt and they cannot allow people to withdraw their money out of the banks. This is all very amazing to me. The same thing is on the horizon for America as far as I can see, the high gas prices and food prices testify of this. At this moment the pain is such that it does not spark the alarm of the population to go out into the street and to hold the government authorities responsible. The pain has not reached that level as of yet but it is surely coming. For some reason America can afford to give billions of dollars to Ukraine to fund the hostilities going on between the Ukraine and Russia. But America cannot afford to lower the high prices of all things or to figure out a way to fix the supply chain issues currently plaguing the American economy. The real answer is the agenda of depopulation and what is called in the media of the great reset. Europe has an even more pressing problem coming this winter because of the sanctions against Russia and Russia retaliating with decreased gas supply to Europe. Europe must be one of the dumbest countries ever to exist to shoot themselves in the foot by agreeing to sanction Russia to the point that they now must deal with the lack of oil and gas they will suffer this coming winter. It is clear that we have entered into a fatal riptide economically. Will all this really go on to its fatal conclusion?

Is anyone listening?

Its easy

It's easy
It's easy
If inside of you
the spirit

To do right
To give glory
To give honor
To the God on high

Is foreign
In your mind
And darkness
In the place
Where there should be

Truth and light
It's easy
It's easy
To live a lie

To deceive the people
To openly confess
An evil agenda
Over and over again

When will
The powers that be
Understand
Lies and deception

They have an end

But on you go
You evil demons
Calling yourself
Workers of good

Doctors and physicians
Introducing
Variant after variant
Virus after virus

Corona after corona
To scare and frighten
The young and defenseless
Well meaning mothers

But their trust
You took
Advantage of
Every four months

More shots needed
For the purpose of
The immune system
To be defeated

No, you won't say it
Though you know it's true

Such evil I'm sure
Even takes the God of all things
By surprise
In its depth and scope

This ongoing agenda
Vaccination after vaccination
Tear down the Georgia guidestones
The people too well informed

But keep the lie going
The people do nothing
They fear God
We the evil do not

So, what do we care
About the law of

To harm do not?
The air we breathe

The ground we walk
The food we eat
Not enough
To go around

It's easy
It's easy
To us
the world belongs
The spoils
to the strong

Depopulation our song
Chattel slavery our goal
Fear and fright
To daily make you comply

It's easy
It's easy
Your soul
Nowhere in sight

To subdue the world
For so short a time
You do not mind
You do not consider

All that is
Say you to yourself
The evil the powers that be
Is what is here and now

Cincinnati of ohio

Sometimes
Around this time of year
I take me back
Cincinnati of OH

Overview ln

Land of long ago

My early years
In the summertime
In July
Birthday month

of my brother
Charles Jr the great
And the greatest cousin
Known to man

My Lionel
Lionel Abrams
I remember
Cincinnati of Ohio

In the summertime
muggy hanging air
the smell of skin
In the night

No girl by my side

Or the others
Of my type
basketball in hand
Three to a side

First team to five

8:00 o'clock
Or 9:30
Same thing
Sitting on the curb

Me and my friend

Or in the car
Barely running
You needed a friend
Who was a mechanic

In order to drive it
For a few minutes
In Cincinnati of Ohio
In the summertime

At night

No school
Or homework
At sunrise

Gas a foreign thing
$0.50 a gallon
Too much money
When your Hebrew

young man

Living in the city

Thick sweat
Under my arms
I hated that
But nature

too powerful

In Cincinnati

Of Ohio
A young Hebrew

Man child

In the promised land
No promise of success
Better find a way

Or else...

To make it
Yourself
no help

Save the God of
Abraham
Isaac
Jacob

Life a constant test
In Cincinnati
Of Ohio
Trying to find

Myself

Watching the white man
Prosper and shout
Getting degreed
But my people

Minimum wage
In Cincinnati
Of Ohio
Where my dad

Running for office
Of Mayor

Without success
Cincinnati of Ohio
Not ready
For social progress

So, he chose
To sit
On the Cincinnati
School board instead

At least when it came
To people of color
In the summertime
Politics don't matter

In august
The air is hot
And muggy
At the same time

Bet be Guzzlin
Malt Liquor

All 40oz
All your life
In the Nati
In the summertime

If you wanna
Stay alive
Cold and sweaty
Big bottles

Hit songs of the 70s

Parliament
Aqua boogie
All in my mind
Feet doin a slide

Torn jeans
And short skirts
Terrible thing
Too afraid to flirt

In the summertime
Big green trees
The cool shade
Cincinnati of Ohio
Bee stings

Fastball rising
breaking mitts
Batters swing

And miss...

In the summertime
In my high school of life
Afro hair
Up high

Jump shots
All net
From the sky

Getting a buzz
Off of a dollar and a dime
In the summertime
In the Cincinnati

Of the Ohio
Of my life

Mens hearts failing them

I am a fisher of men. I am seeking Hebrew Israelites, sons and daughters of light, for fellowship and for the purpose of me ministering to you by way of posting scripture in my room on Facebook, in hopes that you might evolve to want to do ministry, or if you need daily encouragement, and help focusing on spiritual things, then I try to help with that too.

I write books, if you type in my nation yaiquab yisrael on Amazon my books should come up, where I basically try to write about my experiences in this reality from a Hebrew Israelite perspective. I have a dream to establish a nationwide ministry, ministering to other less fortunate Israelites, especially women and children by way of a food ministry. Contact me if you know of anyone who could use assistance, and I will proclaim it on my programs in hopes that someone nearby may be able to minister to the brother or sister.

 The name of the program tonight is "Men's hearts failing them" for fear of those things coming on the earth, as stated in the Gospel of Luke. There is a guarantee in the world. We will see the fear of lord, and that my brothers and sisters is a promise. All the oppressors of the Negro will see the fear of the lord, all the oppressors of the Negro of the Latino of the Native American, on their father's side, will see the fear of the Lord. That is a promise. The oppressors of the Hebrew Israelites will pay a very grievious price. And that is a promise. It might not seem like it at the moment. But it will come to pass. It is the great, ugly secret the nations do not want to know about because, they have used us. They have sold us they have profited off of us. They have shed our blood raped our women, divided our families stolen our identity removed us from our land and the heavenly father, the God of Abraham, Isaac and Jacob has not forgotten even one of the smallest drops of blood that have been spilled by the oppressor nations.

The Heavenly Father has not forgotten the smallest injustice in the most darkest secret place, wherever in the world that has happened against the children of Israel. There is a guarantee in the world. We will see the fear of the Lord. The Israelites will give thanks and praise the nations of the world will mourn because immediately when Messiah manifest himself, all doubt will cease. As to who his people are. All the blasphemy. All the injustice, all the killing and murder of the Hebrew Israelites. will cease, according to Ezekiel, chapter 25, verse 14, and men's hearts will fail them for fear of what is coming on the earth.

And my brothers and sisters, that is a promise. I want you to behold the downfall of our oppressors happening right now. In our reality. Maybe not fast enough for some of us Israelites. Behold, the affliction of the oppressor nations as they speak of a political solution to the conflagration between Russia and Ukraine. They really don't want a political solution. Europe and the United States want war with Russia. Because we economically have reached the end of our rope. I want to state my predictions for the immediate future to the conclusion of our captivity. I have been hearing disturbing reports of war in August, between Russia and the United States. That there will be some sort of conflagration that will kick it off. And during the fall elections, I perceive the internal civil war of the United States will begin when the Republicans take the House and the Senate and they will immediately begin investigations into the corruption of the Biden administration. And the corruption of their son, Hunter Biden and his corrupt business dealings. investigations will shed light on the fact that the President is involved in influence peddling, selling the office of the president for profit.

Now, let me digress for a second if I may, if anyone is listening, in if I were granted the dainties of the world. I do not perceive, outside of the grace of God that I would be able to withstand the temptations that would happen to me if I were in a position of power, and great authority, I do not count myself any better than the corrupt politicians that we see. And that rule over us, if I were to be honest with myself, in my fallen nature, I have weaknesses. I have not overcome 100%. Even though I do not have anywhere near the number of opportunities to be corrupt as those who are corrupt. I admit that. I have character flaws. I am easily convicted of sin by anyone who knows me, and I would not defend myself because the heavenly Father knows all, and it is worse to lie against the truth.

I believe that is why it is so important that we examine ourselves and we are careful before we throw stones at fallen man in this current reality when we consider ourselves, we are no better. Now the problem I do have with the corrupt powers that be is they refuse to relinquish their position of power. They hold on to their position and the office to which they were entrusted. That is my grievance against the powers that be they will not step aside out of shame and the knowledge that these things are done in the face of the God of Abraham, Isaac and Jacob. That is the problem i have with people who proclaim themselves to be public servants. There will be an uprising in this country when the truth about the stolen elections come out when the Republicans take power this fall and that will be one of the great broken pillars that will bring about the demise of America. The truth about the current virus and the shots in the arm will come under the light of investigation. Anthony Fauci will be found out for his part of implementing global destruction on the kingdom of men and others like him will be brought to justice and could possibly face the death penalty.

The Heavenly Father is going to bring all evil to light that is what I see in the foreseeable future. Brethren, our life is an opportunity. You Hebrew Israelites sons of light our life is for the purpose of redeeming the time and storing up treasure. We have the opportunity to give a witness to build our testimony. All things are yours who work while it is day. Read Psalm 34 Seven. Brethren, how will we escape if we neglect so great a salvation?.

Here the word of the Lord in the book of Zephaniah chapter one. Starting in verse two, "I will utterly consumed all things from off the land saith the Lord, I will consume man and beast I will consume the fowls of the heaven and the fishes of the sea, and the stumbling blocks with the wicked. I will cut off man from off the land saith the Lord. I will also stretch out my hand upon Judah, and upon all the inhabitants of Jerusalem. I will cut off the remnant of baal from this place and the name of the chemarins with the priest and them that worship the host of heaven upon the house tops and them that worship and swear by the Lord and that swear by Malcham and them that are turned back from the lord and those that have not sought the Lord, nor inquired for him. Hold thy peace at the presence of the Lord God for the day of the Lord is at hand for the Lord have prepared a sacrifice. He hath bid his guest, And it shall come to pass in the day of the Lord's sacrifice, that I will punish the princess and the king's children and all such as are clothed with strange apparel. In the same day also, will I punish all those that leap on the threshold which fill their masters houses with violence and deceit Verse 10, And it shall come to pass in that day. saith the LORD, that there shall be the noise of a cry from the fish gate and and howling from the second and a great crashing from the hills. Verse 12 Jumping down to verse 12. And it shall come to pass at that time that I will search Jerusalem with candles and punish the men that are settled on their lees that say in their heart, the Lord will not do good. Neither will He do evil. Verse 14, the great day of the Lord is near. It is near and hasteth greatly. Even the voice of the day of the Lord. The mighty man shall cry there bitterly. That day is a day of wrath, a day of trouble and distress, a day of wasteness and desolation, a day of darkness and gloominess a day of clouds and thick darkness, a day of the trumpet and alarm against the fencde cities and against the high towers.

And I will bring distress upon men that they show walk like blind men because they have sinned, against the Lord. And their blood shall be poured out as dust and their flesh as the dung neither their silver nor their gold shall not be able to deliver them in the day of the Lord's wrath but the whole land shall be devoured by the fire of His jealousy, for he shall make even a speedy riddance of all that dwell in the land.

Brethren, we are in that time right now. And because judgment is very subtle, even though it is a loud trumpet. It does not resonate with the men of this world. That all the confluence of events to bring down the kingdom of man is by the will of the God of Abraham, Isaac and Jacob. The Heavenly Father is allowing those of our nation even to remain asleep until he moves his finger and it is too late to seek after the God of Abraham, Isaac and Jacob to build your testimony to be a light.

 Please join me Wednesday and Friday 8pm Pacific Standard Time.
Send me a friend invite on Facebook.
Come and have fellowship let's Redeem the time right now.
Until I see you again.
Peace be until you

shalom

BECAUSE OF THY VIOLENCE

And this is the Israelite, sons of light radio program that I like to try to do every Wednesday and Friday. Thank you for joining me before I begin, I want to give thanks to my Heavenly Father earthly mother for giving me this incredible opportunity to realize what I should do with my life. And the energy that I have been given to draw near to the God of Abraham, Isaac, and Jacob. Truly, truly, I believe I am really blessed to be able to minister in this way.

Now this is a ministry for Hebrew Israelites. I have a room on Facebook for fellowship called the upper room. You can send me a friend and fight on Facebook. And hopefully I'll get a chance to talk to you and let you see how we operate in the room. What the room is all about. I would like to try to help brothers to do ministry but if not the goal of my room is to simply help you to bear fruit on a daily basis to help you to stay focused on things above by posting of scripture from different books. That is my objective. Now I'm also an author and you can go to Amazon and type in my name yaiquab Yisrael and my books should come up. I have a website called twelvetribesisraelites.com all lowercase letters spelled together. Now I have a dream of a nationwide ministry, ministering to our brothers and sisters, especially sisters with children who have a food need, my desire is to come into contact with someone who has a food need so that I may come before the nation and make a supplication in case someone is nearby who can minister to the brother or sister someone who is less fortunate? Contact me. Give me the state and the city and I will proclaim it to the nation that we have a brother or a sister who has a food need and to ask our nation anyone nearby to minister to the brother or sister. Just contact me and then I can take it from there. Now the name of the program tonight is "because of thy violence".

Now, brothers and sisters you may have noticed the confluence of events going on in the world today. Now this is not by coincidence. It is judgment. It is the Heavenly Father bringing recompense because of the way the oppressor nations have treated us have treated his word have lived deliciously. While the Hebrew Israelites have been suffering, an affliction of vexation and oppression at the hands of the oppressor nations. Messiah said to pray that we escape the things coming on the earth and really are already here. Such as vaccinations, such as wars. and rumors of wars. These things are already here. And we are supposed to be praying that we can escape the things coming on the earth. The scripture says the righteous will scarcely be saved. Meaning barely by the skin of our teeth. That is the seriousness of the time that we are in right now. We should be able to see the judgment closing in on the world. I recall seeing a video called Operation Looking Glass. I believe I spoke about it. A few videos back where esau was able to develop technology I believe in the early 2000s that could help him no one what was coming in the future. It was called "Operation looking glass". So that you can go online and check it out. For yourself. To make a long story short, they had to shut down the project because all the timelines that they fed into the computer lead to one conclusion which was the end of this reality.

The machine that they developed predicted one event coming on the earth based on the information that they fed into the computer. The computer was able to come up with a conclusion of what would happen in our current reality. The information was so devastating. They closed the project down, the computer predicted there was nothing that man would be able to do to avoid what was coming on the earth. Did anyone hear about China warning?. The United States if Nancy Pelosi visits Taiwan, that they will respond with forceful measures?. Did anyone see the video? Of Hunter Biden's diary and how he hates his dad? If you ever get to see that video, it is amazing because he really, I believe is crying out that he is corrupted and he blames his dad. He really shows in that diary. How he hates his father.

Brethren, the situation in Europe is another time clock. The Russian president is threatening to cut off gas to Europe which will not allow them to heat their homes in the winter. It is a very dire situation. It is a situation that can only conclude in war, most likely nuclear war. Every day Russia gains more and more ground over the Ukraine the army is slowly advancing and eventually we'll take the whole country. This will force Europe to do something. They are trying to figure out a way to go to war with Russia. They are doing this by trying to add Ukraine to NATO so that they will have an excuse to go to war with Russia. Because the NATO charter states that if one country goes to war all NATO countries go to war. Anyone listening to the sound of my voice should know that all these things has come upon the Edomite kingdoms simply because of the way they have treated Israel. The 12 tribes the historical injustice revelation six three is the opening of a seal predicting food shortage and high inflation and the impossibility of being able to survive financially because of the high price of the basics of life. A denarius for a quart of wheat and three pennies for barley, a quart of barley. Brethren, anybody who is looking for Messiah will easily see these things coming on the earth. Messiah said that to those that look for him he will appear without spot or wrinkle. The bride looks for Messiah. Messiah lets us know the nearness of our restoration. By the current confluence of events, it is meant for our encouragement. It is meant for our Preparing to prepare to meet our God, all these things are coming upon the Edomites kingdoms and japhetic kingdoms because of the way they have treated the Hebrew Israelites and even to this day they do not know why these judgments are coming upon the earth they do not know their best chance of receiving even a crumb of mercy is to acknowledge their sin against the 12 tribes of Israel. But the Heavenly Father does not give them the knowledge to do so. So, they go on and on afflicting us, oppressing us, lying to us implementing agendas to depopulate us so therefore, they make their judgment worse.

Behold, the word of the Lord and the book of Obadiah. The vision of Obadiah thus saith the Lord God concerning Edom. We have heard a rumor from the Lord and Ambassador is sent among for heathen arise up and let us rise up against her in battle. Behold, I have made thee small among the heathen thou are greatly despise the pride of thine heart have deceived thee thou that dwells in the clefs of the rock, whose habitation is high, that saith in his heart Who shall bring me down to the ground?. Though thou exalt thyself as the eagle and though thou set thy nest among the stars, I will bring thee down saith the Lord, if these came to thee if robbers by night How are they cut off? Would they not have stolen till they had enough? If the grape gatherers came to thee would they not leave some grapes? in other words, Esau He takes everything and leaves nothing behind. His system takes everything and leaves nothing behind. Verse six, how are the things of Esau searched out? How are his hidden things sought up? All the men of thy confederacy have brought the even to the border. The men that were at peace with the have deceived thee and prevail against thee they that eat thigh bread have laid a wound under the there is none understanding in him.

Now, if you were to ask me, I would say this is talking about primarily America and Europe. Verse eight, shall I not in that day saith the Lord even destroyed the wise men out of Edom and understanding out of the mouth of Esau. This is an interesting verse, because the sanctions that America and Europe applied against Russia has backfired to where Russian GDP has greatly increased because of the sanctions and other nations are buying Russian oil and gas for cheap. The wisdom of America and Europe has been destroyed and they have too much pride to repent to try to make peace and put an end to the current situation. That is why the conflict between Russia and Ukraine can only reach one conclusion. NATO and America must go to war with Russia. The American dollar is greatly destroyed because Saudi Arabia is using other currencies to sell their oil in and no longer using the dollar exclusively. This means a perilous situation for America. We cannot continue to print money when nobody will trade in our currency. Verse nine and thy mighty men Oh Teman shall be dismayed to the end that everyone of the mount of Esau may be cut off by slaughter. Now what does that mean to anyone under the sound of my voice? does it sound like a nuclear war that Esau will be cut off by? verse 10 For thy violence against thy brother Jacob, shame shall cover thee and thou shalt be cut off forever because of the historical violence and the slavery and even till this day depopulation programs by way of the needle, if you know what I mean. Shame shall cover esau for their violence against Jacob, the 12 tribes of Israel all these things are coming on Esau and Japheth because of their violence towards Jacob. All the confluence of events that are happening right now is because of thy violence against thy brother Jacob. Verse 11 And the day that thou stood is on the other side in the day that the strangers carried away captive his forces and foreigners entered into his gates, and cast lots upon Jerusalem. Even thou was as one of them. But thou should not have looked on the day of thy brother in the day that he became a stranger. Neither should thou have rejoiced over the children of Judah, and the day of their destruction. neither shouldest thou have spoken proudly in the day of distress, talking about when we fell in slavery, and the scripture that says, Blessed be the Lord, for I am rich. That's what they said, when they realized that we had been handed over to the oppressor nations. Verse 14, neither should thou have stood in the crossway to cut off those of his that did escape. Neither should thou have delivered up those of his that did remain, and the day of distress for the day of the Lord is near, upon all the heathen as thou has done, it shall be done unto thee. Thy reward shall return upon thy own head. For as you have drunk upon my holy mountain, so shall all the heathen drink continually, yea, they shall drink, and they shall swallow down and they shall be as though they have not been but upon mountain zion shall be deliverance, and there shall be holiness, and the house of Jacob shall possess their possessions. And the house of Jacob shall be a fire and house of Joseph, a flame and House of Esau for stubble. And they show Kindle in them and devour them, and there shall not be any remaining of the house of Esau for the Lord has spoken it and they of the south shall possess the mount of Esau, and the plane the Philistines and they shall possess the fields of Ephraim, and the fields of Samaria and Benjamin shall possess Gilead and the captivity of the souls of the children of Israel shall possess that canaanites even unto zarepath, and the captivity of Jerusalem, which is sefirat shall possess the cities of the south and Saviordthe shall come upon Mount Zion, to judge the mount of esau, and the kingdom shall be the Lord's brethren, all things are ours. All things will belong to the Hebrew Israelites. Even the oppressor nations, that heavenly father even now is beginning to bring judgment against them. For thy violence against my brother Jacob.

 Join me Wednesday and Friday 8pm Pacific Standard Time
on the Israelites radio program
until I see you again,
peace be unto you,
Shalom.

Precious sons

The precious sons
Noticed by no one
Esteemed as forsaken
But spiritually

They are
The precious sons
Of Zion

Living in
The beast Kingdom
Of men
A Kingdom numb

Of any
Spiritual inclination
No respect at all
Or fear

Of the God of
Abraham
Of Isaac
Of Jacob

A Kingdom
A beast Kingdom
Daily overcoming
The only carriers of light

Pointing the way
To fellowship
To peace and love
The precious sons

Of Zion

Comparable to find gold
But esteemed as earthen vessels

The precious sons
Of Zion
To whom one day
The earth will bow
And recompense made
For any and all crimes

To execute a judgment
On the great and the small
Who gave no thought
To the Kingdom of God

The precious sons
Of Zion
A day will come
In which the precious sons

Will shine their light
Seven times the brightness
Of the sun

Presently residing
In earthen vessels
In heart and soul
Which is

The eternal spirit
The spirit of God
These are
The precious sons

Of Zion

Russia is a man

I had a very interesting thought today which was this, the nation of Russia has the spirit of a man. Russia is currently at odds with Europe and the United states primarily through a proxy war with Ukraine. Russia does not have a lot of women's leaders. Russia is a man's man type of state. Russia is more in line with the Bible than the United states which claims the Bible as the only word of God. The Bible says the heavenly father does not suffer a woman to rule over a man and I firmly believe one of the reasons that America will fall and Europe as well is because they have not cared about the heavenly order of relations between men and women. America is filled with women leaders and Europe as well. They do not realize that this is a cause for the judgment that is now falling upon this nation. They do not realize this is one of the reasons that judgment is coming upon this nation leading to its ultimate demise. Feminism has divided this country into male and female camps even till this day constantly the media makes an issue of the differences between male and female to our own demise. Russia is a nation that understands a man's place is to stand in rulership over his people Russia also seems to understand the fear of God and the importance of being on the right side of history. And for this the heavenly father will use Russia to bring final judgment on America and Europe. To me it is obvious that you cannot go against the decreed heavenly order of the God of Abraham Isaac and Jacob and prosper and this is a lesson America has yet to learn but must learn the hard way.

WOMEN LEADERS

I try to minister on a daily basis in hopes of helping you to evolve to do ministry, or to just help you on a daily basis to try to focus on spiritual things and things of the God of Abraham, Isaac and jacob. I want to share a dream that I have of ministry in a food sense to our nation, primarily women with children. A food ministry where I would like to be contacted if someone knows of a brother or sister that has a food need that needs to be ministered to, so that I may bring this information to the nation in case someone nearby may be able to minister to the brother or sister. I have a website twelvetribesisraelites.com all lowercase letter and spelled gather. The name of my room on Facebook is called the upper room. Why don't you join me and let us Redeem the time. Let us store up for ourselves. Let us not give our full energy to the world. The Heavenly Father is certainly showing us without a shadow of a doubt. We do not have much time left at all. With every new day. We are drawing closer and closer to April 2024. When the slant that goes across America when considering the solar eclipse of 2017 will form an "x" across America. Signaling most likely a terrific event most likely the end of this current reality. So, this is something we should take very seriously. While it is day when we can work and we can build up and store up and allow our works to save us.

The Scripture say that we should pray that we will escape the things coming on the earth. Recently, I have been reminded of one of the reasons why America is coming under great, great judgment. The title of my program tonight is "women leaders", women leaders. Now I am positive that people can make a great case for women leaders and there have been women leaders and our nation. Now, that was the exception and not the rule. We have been taken captive to the oppressor nations whose system of governance is to allow women ruling over men now currently, we have a vice president in office right now who is soon to become President of the United States due to the declining condition of President Biden, who has been diagnosed with dementia and is showing strong symptoms by making nonsensical statements making incorrect speech facts not being able to read the teleprompter correctly by referring to things that have no bearing on what the question at hand was. This is something that he does on a daily basis whenever he is giving a press conference and if the Republicans take the House and the Senate if he last that long, he will be heavily investigated. He will be found guilty of influence peddling along with his son and he will be removed that way. And Kamala Harris will become president one way or another. We will have a woman president at a time we have never seen before. To me it is obvious that this thing is been orchestrated by the Heavenly Father, if it isn't enough, that Kamala Harris middle name is devi that is too close to being a non coincidence to me that the Heavenly Father is showing us a prophecy through her name that she is a spawn of Satan.

Now, I could be wrong, but it seems to me the Heavenly Father raised her up so that the whole world will not be able to deny that we have flipped the order of the God of Abraham, Isaac and Jacob and basically slapped him in the face by taking the cosmic order of the relationship between a man and a woman and despising it even to this day. She will, in my humble opinion, be President of the United States at a time when we will see nuclear war and the confluence of events testify to that fact.

America and Europe has an abundance of women ruling over men while Russia does not. Russia is a very manly type of nation. If we recall the Scriptures we read in Genesis, the Bible says that thy desire, speaking of the woman shall be towards thy husband, but he shall rule over thee. Now this is very interesting, because in my personal experience, almost down to every woman I have dealt with, they have one way or another sought to rule over me. There seems to be a spirit, at least at the female principle that I have encountered. There seems to be a love of the world a love of luxury, a love of power. There seems to be as the Scriptures say, a weakness that the female principal has. She is described as the weaker sex. Now Christianity and Catholicism to me are heavily to blame as well with their agenda of the love doctrine, with their agenda of female Liberation with their agenda of erasing the memory of the God of Abraham, Isaac, and Jacob. The scripture in John chapter 10, verse 35, says" the word cannot be broken", meaning you cannot use the New Testament against the Old Testament. They harmonize with one another. The Christians like to say the New Testament is what they follow as if the Old Testament has been done away with, which we, as Hebrew Israelites know that is a lie. The Lord says, I am the Lord and I change not the oppressor nations surrounding us, have deceived us and taught us not to be concerned about the God of Abraham, Isaac, and Jacob. And this thing has worked, nowhere unless you were fortunate enough to find a Hebrew, Israelite son or daughter of light, speak of the God of Abraham, Isaac, and Jacob. The agenda is for the powers that be to erase his memory. Like it says in Psalm 83 this agenda has thoroughly been successful in our day and age. The powers that be mainly Christianity, and Catholicism has given our nation women leaders, abortions, pornography, for the purpose of the breakdown of Hebrew Israelite nuclear family structure. The female principal is described as the weaker sex so that is where the enemy will attack our nation. The stronger adversary always attacks at a weakest point of their strongest adversary. So, he attacks us through the female principal. Do you remember the story of Samson and delilah and how the enemies of Israel used Delilah to find the secret of Samson's strength? It is the same way today.

The oppressor nations mainly the people of revelation two nine and three nine operate from the same playbook to compromise men in order to instill their agenda in order to implement their own agenda. Now, most of you probably have never heard of Adam weishaup. He is a founder of the Illuminati. Now, one of the objectives of the Illuminati was to subdue male domination through the female by appealing to the woman's sense of vain glory by feeding her the theory that she should not be subject to the rule of men. And that is how women's liberation eventually bore fruit in the 1970s, starting from the 1700s Adam wieshaupt belongs to the people of revelation two, nine and Revelation three nine.

The philosophy that he put forward is for creating a society where women can weaken men through the promise and illusion of sex, and immodestly clothing themselves for the purpose of inciting lust in a man and this poison was eventually spread to our nation. That Hebrew Israelites were infected with this theory that this revelation two nine revelation three nine man put fourth and it worked. The Illuminati called for an attack on biblical morality. Men authority figures became weakened in their character and begin to compromise themselves because of the weakness of their flesh. And women begin to take authority over a man and the Illuminati took advantage of the woman's weakness to the luxury, to the power to the vain glory, that they gave them. And now you have what we have today. The Heavenly Father has been totally disrespected his order has been flipped. It was never changed. Now the time has come for the judgment and recompense for this and many other things. The God of Abraham, Isaac and Jacob has forgotten none of these things, the secret agendas to subdue the Hebrew Israelites 1000s of generations, even up till now of our captivity. So, since you would not respect his cosmic order, and the decree he has set forth for our own benefit, and the relationship between men and women, but because you have corrupted the oppressor nations have corrupted the Hebrew Israelites and also leading them to flip the cosmic order on his head. Therefore, hear ye the Word of the Lord in Jeremiah 25.

And it shall come to pass when 70 years or accomplish that I will punish the king of Babylon. And that nation saith the Lord for their iniquity, and the land of the chaldeans, and we'll make it perpetual desolations and I will bring upon that land, all by words, which I have pronounced against it. Even all that is written in this book, which Jeremiah have prophesied against all the nations, for many nations, and great kings shall serve themselves of them, (meaning they would serve themselves of the Israelites). And I will recompense them according to their deeds, and according to the works of their own hands. For thus saith the Lord God of Israel, unto me, take the wine cup of this fury at my hand, and cause all the nations to who I send thee to drink it and they shall drink and be moved and be mad because of the judgment that I will send among them. Then took I the cup, at the Lord's hand, and make all nations to drink, unto whom the Lord had sent me, starting with us, judah Jerusalem, in the cities of Judah and the kings thereof and the princess thereof to make them a desolation and astonishment and hissing and purse as it is to this day. Pharaoh, king of Egypt and his servants and his princes and all his people and all the mingled people and all the kings of the land of us and all the kings of the land of the Philistines and Ashkelon, and Asia. And Ekron. And the remnant of Ashdod, and Moab, and the children of Ammon and all the kings of Tartarus all the kings of Sidon and the kings of the isles which are beyond the sea dedan and teman and buzz, and all that are in the isles, far corners, jumping down. Therefore, thou shalt say to them thus saith the LORD of hosts, the God of Israel drink and be drunken, and spew and fall and rise no more, because of the sword which I will send among you, and it shall be if they refuse to take the cup, then thou shalt say unto them, Thus saith the LORD of hosts, ye shall certainly drink for lo, I begin to bring evil on the city, which is called by my name, and should you be utterly unpunished? you shall not be unpunished for I will call for a sword upon all the inhabitants of the earth. saith the LORD, host Therefore prophesy thou against them, all these words, and say unto them, The Lord shall roar from on high, and utter his voice, from his holy habitation, he shall mightily roar upon his habitation he shall give a shout, as they that tread the grapes against all the inhabitants of the earth.

A noise shall come even to the ends of the earth. For the Lord has a controversy with the nation's he will judge with all flesh. He will give them that are wicked to the sword saith the Lord, thus saith the Lord of hosts. Behold, evil shall go forth from nation to nation, and a great whirlwind shall be raised up from the coast of the earth. And the slain of the Lord shall be at that day, from one end of the earth even unto the other end of the earth. They shall not be lamented. Neither gathered, nor buried, they shall be dung upon the ground. Howl you shepherds and cry and wallow yourselves in the ashes, ye principle of the flock. For the days of your slaughter, and of your dispersions are accomplished, and ye shall fall like a pleasant vessel and the shepherds shall have no way to flee, nor the principle of the flock, to escape, a voice of the cry of the shepherds and howling of the principle of the flock, shall be heard, for the lord hath spoiled their pasture, and peaceable habitations are cut down because of the fierce anger of the Lord. He has forsaken his covert as the lion, for their land is desolate, because of the fierceness of the oppressor and because of his fierce anger. So go ahead America, fill up the cup. You are under a great judgment for governing the Israelites under a system that allows the female principal to rule over men. For this. Your male principle will pay a mighty price.

Thank you for joining me join me Wednesday and Friday.
Go to my description box. Click on the link to join me my brethren in my room on Facebook.
And for other information in the description box.
Until I see you again want to give thanks to my Heavenly Father earthly mother for this incredible opportunity.
peace be unto you,
Shalom.

Cosmic design

Day after day
The images
Go not away
Broken buildings

Lives and children
Fighting and missiles
Over there
Land of war

Death and destruction
The result of secret planning
And agendas
Bearing full fruit

In this
Day of age

World domination
A current theme
For the current reality
Good against evil

Because some want all
For themselves
Even if
The whole world

 suffers

The children of Satan
Still in their power
Knowing in their heart
Their cosmic decline

Knowing in their heart
There is no place
For human lies

In the eternal plan

But it's too late now
Might as well
Continue implementing
The evil plan

Even to the end
Even if it means
Their own destruction

To bring man
into bondage
No way out
No way to escape

The spirit of love
And freedom
Of the spirit and soul
Far far too great

For the gods
Of this world
To fully dominate
Try as they may

the Negro looks up
He knows his fate
To inherit
The eternal Kingdom

Which never ever
Can fade away

When the word goes out
From our God and father
To end our captivity
And to bring recompense

To the current evil

And bloody agenda
Of evil spirits and angels
Of killing and bloodshed

Robbing the young
Of the opportunity...
To experience the God
Of Abraham Isaac and Jacob

All because of
An evil agenda
Of the powers that be
To destroy and withhold

Life, love
liberty

The brotherhood of man
That creation
was always
Meant to be

Until the fall

Of the cosmic heavenlies

No sooner do I put my writing pen down that I must pick it back up again in order to testify for antiquity sake the things that are happening on a very rapid scale pointing to the eventual conclusion of the experiment called the Kingdom of man.

While watching a video broadcast today the news came out that China is threatening military action against the United States if the speaker of the house Nancy Pelosi goes forward with a visit to Taiwan in the month of August. Whether this will take place or not I do not know at the present. If the United States were smart, they would find a reason to cancel the trip such as a sudden sickness or a last minute and opportune situation that must be attended to.

Anything anything but the threat of a possible nuclear confrontation. But in the present reality there seems to be no more wisdom in the leaders of the United States or in Europe as anyone should be able to see they are constantly legislating and acting against their own best interests.

Barring an act of God Europe will face a dire winter of 2022 because of their participation in the sanctions against Russia which have backfired. It does not appear to Europe that the United States loves proxy wars. As long as the foreign nations are willing to endure the pain of the policies put forth by the United States that will be just fine with America. Europe and the Ukraine have not figured that out yet, so they are willing to suffer a disastrous economic and geopolitical final destruction to themselves.

For someone like me I know what all this means, I continue to watch every day with absolute astonishment amazement that all this is really going on. I am in a daily state of shock that the powers that be meaning the American hegemony is so willing to destroy the only Kingdom they will have. They are willing to do this because they do not believe in the eternal Kingdom the God of Abraham Isaac and Jacob, where there will exist righteousness holiness and judgment.

The American hegemony only believes in itself and no one else and this blindness is exactly the reason for the vortex of decline that I am currently witnessing in this reality today and it is a most amazing thing. So now we sit and wait to see what will become of the speaker of the house Nancy Pelosi and her visit to Taiwan.

Count me worthy

My father
Who art heaven
I need help
The world I live in

Every day
Trying to steal
The light within me
Telling me

You are not real
Unworthy to be believed
Unworthy to be feared
Unworthy to be loved

Oh, my father
I pray your help
That I may escape
This fallen world

And the evil
Ever increasing
I thank you my father
Showing me

The time
running out
The nearness of your Kingdom

The blessing of the Saints
Forever

I am alone
In my reality
Having no one
To confide in

To take comfort in

And the power
of your word
There is no testimony
In my acquaintances

They speak not of
The God of Abraham
Of Isaac
Or Jacob

Having eyes
That cannot see
Only flesh
Carnal senses

And desires

That is where I live
So, my father
Who art heaven
Please count me worthy

To escape
When the blindness
you lift
Revealing great power

And glory

Oh, my father
Count me worthy
To escape
Having this testimony

My desire
To work
While it is day
While forgiveness

Still near

Remember Me my father
For good
Not evil
Remember Me

To count me worthy

Sri Lanka

June 23rd, 2022, the Sri Lankan government collapsed for some reason the Prime Minister of that nation decided not to leave well enough alone and ordered the nations farmers to stop using herbicides and pesticides when planting their crops which caused a nearly overnight 50% reduction in crop harvest disastrously affecting their export abilities, crashing their economy. Just as the British Prime Minister resigned and the Italian Prime Minister government also collapsed with France most likely to follow, all because of the current hostilities going on between Russia and Ukraine greatly caused by America using Europe to do its bidding in America's effort to weaken Russia. Is it really possible to conclude this not being the judgment of the God of Abraham Isaac and Jacob? If you are reading this and you have little food, no money no job no idea where your next meal is coming from you probably live in Sri Lanka right now. I do not believe in coincidences. I believe this is another example of how the God of Abraham Isaac and Jacob brings judgment. In our nation we do not care about Sri Lanka or other governments in America we care more if the local fast-food restaurant closes down then you will see riots in the street that is the value system of America, just keep the dainties coming we don't care how you get them here you just keep it coming. And the government knows this so they make sure they cater to the flesh of man while implementing agendas to make him a slave knowing that America will be satisfied with being provided for their basic needs even if it means the loss of their freedom loss of their faith loss of their finances and loss of their dignity. America does not care. Just so long as ignorance of the God of Abraham Isaac and Jacob persist all is well in America.

Sri Lanka is a Canary in a coal mine, a precursor to what is coming upon the Western Hemisphere. An ominous warning of revelation chapter 6 verse 3 Sri Lanka is a precursor to the fall of many governments. Caucasian led governments. Sri Lanka used to be a very rich country because of its tourism and its agriculture but now it is destined to be a chattel slave state for its foreseeable future. Why has this judgment come on the people of Sri Lanka? They seem like a pretty peaceable good people to me, I do not know what God they worship, and I know that the curse does not come for no reason at all. I do know from reading that the president and previous leaders of that country have made terrible decisions regarding their economy also in part due to the corruption that comes with consolidated power within a family, and I do know they have suffered from terrorism scaring tourists away from their country. But for whatever reason we are being shown what is coming to us, but we do not believe it. But to me this is exactly in line with how the heavenly father warns the children of Israel the Hebrew Israelites to forsake the world and its lies and godlessness.

To me the events of the fall of different governments is a way the heavenly father warns the world to prepare to give an account for the life he has given to man and his Kingdom. But we cannot hear we cannot respond in a spiritual way.

 America is being led to a slaughter because of the historical forsaking of the knowledge of the God of Abraham Isaac and Jacob even with this understanding I still cannot believe the confluence of events that have been in effect for at least 2019 until the present and the future does not look any better with the advent of the planet Pluto concluding its cycle of death and rebirth in 2024 and the "X" that will finish forming across America with a solar eclipse in 2024 of April. Messiah said to watch, and Messiah said to those that look for him shall he appear Messiah, Messiah said Matthew 24 will come, these are different ways that we who are the bride of Messiah can see the end of our captivity.

The apathy in this current reality even amongst the nation of the Hebrew Israelites is an amazing thing. The drive to survive has replaced the desire to draw near to the God of Abraham Isaac and Jacob. I am willing to presume that the people of Sri Lanka are having the biggest prayer meetings they have ever had to their God at this particular moment. I cannot imagine the daily prospect of trying to decide how you will feed your family when there is nothing to feed them with and there is no solution insight. That is the plight of the people of Sri Lanka right now. Governments are falling, nations are fighting, the God of Abraham and Isaac and Jacob is waiting. The secret depopulation agenda is raging but even all these things and more is not enough to cause the nation worlds to consider the eternal Kingdom of the Hebrew Israelites and it's imminency.

Pondering

Today I saw a man
And I considered him
Gray of hair
Soft of eye

Slowly he walked
Both hands joined
behind his back
pensive

in his demeanor

And I beheld him
And I considered
in my mind
More than likely

He was considering
His mortality

To me
At least

It seems…

From the time
Of the age
60 and above
I count it wisdom

If from that time
You begin to consider
The lessons learned
Of our lives given

And I beheld him
He walked

very slowly
Most of the time
Considering
the ground before him

But I knew
He was thinking
Considering
What lay before him

Whether he had
redeemed the time
I do not know
A peace did cover him

A peaceful soul
Pondering his past
It was all he had
And he walked along

Hands joined
Behind his back

August 18th

Happy born day day elloria

August 28th

Happy born day Sharon

Fire fire

I believe one of the first things that should be made clear when you believe in worship of the God of Abraham Isaac and Jacob is to serve others. When I look at Messiah, I look at someone who served others. When I first learned that automatically, I knew there was going to be a problem, if I wanted to minister. Immediately I knew in my spirit that I live in a country where people seek out men of goodwill to defraud them, but I learned I was just going to have to trust the spirit. Today was one of those days that I just had to shake my head; a woman called me with her hair on fire wanting me to split the sun for her. The task was impossible… she called me, or should I say contacted me never having talked to me before but having heard me try to minister to my nation on blog talk radio never mind the fact that I was referring to wanting to help provide food for anyone having a food insecurity. All this woman heard was a desire to help which in turn meant to her free money, she was in the process of being evicted THAT DAY and contacted me wanting money to buy a moving van. That is one frustration I have seen trying to minister to Hebrew Israelites they have no relationship with the heavenly father and when their hair catches on fire, they immediately expect someone other than themselves to put the fire out. They have all the time in the world to build a relationship with the heavenly father beforehand but choose not to, and when their house catches on fire, they expect the heavenly father to jump up and run and help them. In my mind the sister got what she deserved the scripture says the curse does not come without a cause proverbs 26. This is something some Israelites do not understand. Even still it made me mad at myself that I was unable to help her because she waited too late, and she ended up blaming me for her situation. If that sister thinks her situation is bad now and if she does not repent and begin to build a relationship with the God of Abraham Isaac and Jacob, then when the wine Press of revelation 14 comes she will not like it

guarantee it.

TESTIFY 4

I hope I didn't frighten you with a new feature I want to add to my program, which is the blowing of the shofar, something we did in our nation to gather the camp and to call upon the God of Abraham, Isaac and Jacob. It was something that the priests did. Thank you for joining me. I want to give thanks to my Heavenly Father earthly mother for this incredible opportunity to be a light while I am in this reality. This is a ministry for Hebrew Israelites, Negros Latinos and Native Americans on their father's side.

I have this ministry so that I may fish for men and women, lively stone, sons and daughters of light, to have fellowship with me and my brethren. On a room I have in Facebook, called the Upper room. I am also an author, you can go to the description box in my YouTube channel for my links in case you are interested in seeing what I write about which is my life and learning about God and people from a Hebrew Israelite perspective, my books are on Amazon, just type in my name and it should lead you to my books, where you have an option to look inside to see the things I write about. I have a website called twelvetribesisraelites.com lowercase letters, all spelled together. For the purpose of you being able to get in contact with me in case anything I say, resonates with you. I also have a dream of establishing a nationwide network of brethren who can assist me if the cry goes out for someone who has food insecurities and needs the basics of food, so that they may get past a rough spot. I want to establish a nationwide Ministry of brethren that I can contact if they are close to the brother or sister in need if you are willing, just send me your city and state to my email. Israelite 94@yahoo.com.

Again, my ministry is for the purpose of being a light to the God of Abraham, Isaac, and Jacob. I titled the name of my program tonight. "Testify part four" a testimony is something you leave behind to speak for you when you are gone. If you look around you in the world today, you will not find a brother testifying of the God of Abraham, Isaac, and Jacob. Chances are you will not meet a brother who will inject into a conversation. Do you know the God of Abraham, Isaac, and Jacob? That is why Messiah said "I shall choose you want of a city two of a family or one of 1000" sons and daughters of light are people who have been elected have been anointed to endure their life being a light to our nation. The Hebrew Israelites for the purpose of testifying of the God of Abraham, Isaac, and Jacob. But as it says in the Gospel of Thomas again, he who has found the world has found a corpse you cannot give testimony of something you do not know of.

Now, anybody who knows me, or has heard me, do my radio programs, knows that I like to use every day analogies to make my point. When talking about the God of Abraham, Isaac, and Jacob there is a Gnostic Saying "as above, so below". It helps us to know how we can understand our overstand the God of Abraham, Isaac, and Jacob, even while we are inside of this corpse called the world.

Now, before I begin, I want to mention something that I forgot to speak about when I opened my program. Now, it concerns the nationwide food ministry. I was contacted by a sister who greatly vexed my soul. And I am sorry to say this has been the case in my dealings with the Hebrew Israelites and trying to minister I have been greatly defeated and disappointed and greatly vexed and afflicted by the things and the Brethren I have dealt with. It lets you know why Messiah said "he did not come to bring peace he came to bring a sword" for the purpose of you sons and daughters of light, to learn to be battle tested and ready to minister and to set aside carnal, earthly feelings when approaching the God of Abraham, Isaac, and Jacob.

Now, a sister contacted me and her hair was on fire. She had heard me proclaim that I wanted to reach out to a brother or sister with my nationwide food ministry. But all she heard was free money. And she contacted me that very day. She told me she was being evicted. And she wanted me to take care of it. By funding her and her husband to get a moving van so that they may pack up and leave and that is actually what happened that very day. I was approached by the sister to put out the fire that I had no idea was raging. She chose the very day when everything had to happen and blamed me for all these problems. When I told her my ministry is geared to helping a brother or sister experiencing food difficulties, for which the sister was angry and blamed me for not helping. Which in turn gave me a fierce attitude at how you brothers and sisters can sometimes be, and it vexed my soul greatly. But I overstand this is the will of God concerning me to endure my reality and give things and give glory and give honor to the God of Abraham, Isaac, and Jacob who promises me and promises you. All things work together for the good for those that love God and are called according to His purpose.

Now, as I've said before, the title of this program is testify now If you were to ask me, if someone told me that they are a son or daughter of the Heavenly Father, but they had no testimony about the reality of the God of Abraham Isaac, and Jacob. I know personally, I would not stick around to listen to that individual for very long. Now I am not saying it should be that way for everyone. There are things we can learn from brothers and sisters without having to follow their example of their character. myself. I tend to gravitate to someone who can speak about the reality of the God of Abraham, Isaac and Jacob in real terms in their life or in a way they can point to. Now I find that I tend to want to testify when a blessing comes my way.

Now yesterday, I went to my mailbox. I found a letter and when I opened it, it said my rent was going down and for the third time in as many years my rent has gone down at a time where there is runaway inflation. High gas, high food and incidentally these things seem to happen to me right after I minister or am given the opportunity to minister to someone and that is what happened. I also testified early last month about the testimony of my minivan and how it happened which was another miracle. I have a place that I live in which is a stone's throw from the ocean. I am a poor man. But I testify to you that I am rich not only in this reality, but also in the eternal kingdom. I want to testify that the way to receiving is giving, the Heavenly Father has given me a life of testimony that I use to feed my soul from when I first started until now.

 I have a testimony that I can share with you both good and bad. Of the things that have happened to me in my life to be a greater light for the God of Abraham, Isaac, and Jacob. And the same should be the case for you, did I ever share with you that if I wanted to. I have no need of even purchasing one stitch of food if I did not want to. Why? Because I receive free food, free food where I live the four food groups meat poultry, dairy, vegetables, snacks they have a garden where I live and it should not take a brilliant, intelligent person to know a blessing when you see one.

A brother or sister who does not testify who has not built a relationship with the Heavenly Father with the God of Abraham, Isaac and Jacob will not be able to testify. So, when the sister called me with her hair on fire, wanting me to split the sun and move mountains for a situation she knew she was headed for because I knew right when she told me that she was in this situation because her relationship with the Heavenly Father was lacking.

I know from reading the scriptures in Proverbs chapter 26, that the curse will not come without a cause. Meaning if sudden affliction, vexation and oppression is in your life. It is there for a reason. Sometimes, these things come about to get you to turn to the Father to draw near. It is a warning. You have not been drawing near. You have not been communing with the angels. You have not been burning incense to the God of Abraham, Isaac and Jacob. You have not been meditating. You have not been praying. You have not struggled to be a light, you have not Minister you have not tried to draw near while it is day so that you may inherit the eternal kingdom as other brothers are doing and gaining the eternal kingdom.

Messiah said my burden is light. He does not give us more than we can handle. If you are in a relationship, you should know if you are dealing with a woman even though you give her maybe 20 or 30% of your best. She will still quadruple your energy by way of her companionship. By way of taking care of you, by way of being in your corner, by way of giving you her beauty, by way of giving you children and raising them.

There is no way to match the love and energy and passion that a sister puts into relationship. It is ordained by God. You can read in the Kolbrin Bible that part of the affliction that she has come under is a heavier responsibility to be in a workable relationship with a man the Heavenly Father is the same way. We cannot match his energy. We cannot give back what he gives to us. If you draw nearer, He will draw near to you. And the opposite is true. You will not be able to testify. If you do not draw near to the God of Abraham, Isaac and Jacob as above so below, do not deceive yourself. God is not mocked whatsoever a man soweth that, will he reap brethren if you have no testimony, it may be because you have no testimony. That is a dangerous thing. Not to have especially at this time, and the confluence of events soon to come upon us. This is a time where we should be praying to escape what is coming on the earth. Now, Heavenly Father willing I will do my next video on the ever-changing confluence of events that concern you, anyone under the sound of my voice that you more than likely have not been hearing about one of the items I plan to bring to your attention is the situation with Evergrande Bank of China. Has anyone ever heard of what is going on with Evergreen Bank of China? and how it will affect the global financial system if it goes into default, already having missed one big payment on a bond. These are things that are happening that we have no idea of that will affect our nation. Brethren, build your testimony. It will testify for you when you leave this current reality.

I want to give thanks to my Heavenly Father earthly mother for this incredible opportunity.

 Join me Wednesday and Friday. Heavenly Father willing 8pm pacific standard time

go to the links in my description box until I see you again. peace be unto you,

Shalom.

Black man

I have to include this in my diary for memory's sake today I met a
Hebrew a Negro a Israelite, and there was a white man standing by and
while the white man was talking he mentioned a black man, so I said to
him what do you mean black man wanting to use the situation to
educate the Hebrew that was standing by. The white man could not
answer what he meant I knew that he was a victim of social
programming implemented by the gods of this world why those who
say they are Jews to slander us by way of this commonly used
pejorative calling the children of Israel black people. So I asked him to
look at the Hebrew brother and tell me what is his literal color the white
man actually said black and I would have strangled him but I restrained
myself. So when I came to I took the opportunity to educate him that he
is not a black man but that he is brown and that the word black is used
as a pejorative against our people and that it has negative connotations.
And to my surprise the brother that I was trying to educate took the side
of the white man saying he did not care what people called him. Upon
hearing this I became troubled for my mental sanity because of dealing
with people like this. It seems our people can be so jaded as to not care
even when the oppressor addresses us by using a pejorative, they
would not do it to messiah, but they will do it to us the children of Israel.
I hope that I can survive this current reality without losing my mind.

pejorative
a noun

pe·jo·ra·tive
: a word or phrase that has negative connotations or that is intended
to disparage or belittle: a pejorative word or phrase

One Thing

One thing I know
One thing it's true
A nuclear weapon
Nothing on earth

More powerful
Except...

The truth
In the hands
Of a Hebrew man
Otherwise known as

A Negro
The twelve tribes

A son of God
Of Abraham
Of Isaac
Of Jacob

One thing I know
This thing is true
A nuclear weapon
Nothing on earth

More powerful
Except...

A Hebrew Israelite
Proclaiming the truth
Of the spiritual kind
Giving praise glory and honor

To the most high

One thing I know
One thing is true

Nothing more powerful
Than a nuclear weapon

Except...
A Hebrew Israelite
Who speaks the truth
Holding his Bible
In full view

In the face of
The oppressor
Who is condemned
By the nuclear weapon

Coming from
The mouth of an Israelite
Destroying all falsehood
Smashing all lies

There is no weapon
To defend against the truth
It must come out
No power on earth

Can deny

Equal in strength
To destroy the spirit
Of the Hebrew oppressor
Even the pride of man

Making his strength
Like water
No ability
To fight against it

When the truth
Spoken by the Hebrew
In full force

And passion
Makes its appearance
Before the oppressor
He trembles

He has no answers
This history
Does not lie
Like the colleges and universities

When it comes
To telling the truth
About the children
Of Israel

Whom the world knows
Must eventually rule
Forever
The Negro, Latino
And Native American

GOVERNMENT AND VOTE

I remember
A while back
My dad
And he asked me

What type
 of governance
 should we have?

But...
I had no answer

At the time

My dad is gone
Too late
To respond
To his question

Very profound

But the answer did come
The government
As best I can tell
For man to have

Is a highly
Unpopular one
So much so
I doubt if

My dad
Would approve of
Likely because
The impracticality

Of such a government

My answer is
A theocratic one
A government
Fearing the God

Of Abraham
Of Isaac
And Jacob
A perfect government

My eternal dilemma
Finding holes
In the current ways
Of man

I remember
Someone asked me
Who would I vote for?
I did not answer

Because I did not
Want Messiah
To be made fun of

So, I declined to answer

And therein lies
My Achilles heel
It keeps me from
Harmonizing

In and with
the beast
Kingdom

A Kingdom of men
Who know not God
Neither fear
His holy name

Why do we complain?
Even though
In our hearts
We know what is true

But no...

On we go
on and on
Refusing
The only way

To live together
In peace and harmony

No theocratic government
No man to stand up
And to give voice about
The God of Abraham

Of Isaac
And Jacob

Hold your peace
Oh, vain man
There will be
A theocratic Kingdom

Messiah as head

And then
I will say to my dad
This is the way

I have always
Felt it should be
It's just that
when you asked me

I was too young
To explain

COLLISION COURSE

The name this program tonight is "collision course". But I don't know how much I will touch on that topic because before I do my videos or meditate and pray and light incense, asking for an anointing on my spirit in order to speak to you now also let me say I am a minister to the Hebrew Israelites, you negros, Latinos, and Native Americans on your father's side. If anything, I say resonates with you. Why don't you go to my YouTube description box and click on the link where there is information for books that I write, I am an author, you can click on the link. I just finished one or I should say will be finished with my latest book in two weeks.

And I have a room on Facebook where you can come and gather and I will do my level best to encourage you and to hopefully help you to evolve to do ministry. If you believe you are lead in that area, anything that I can do by any means to help you to bear fruit. While we are in this reality, just go to the links on my YouTube description box for ministry and information.

Okay, now, as I was saying, I intended to do a prophetical type of program tonight and I may touch on some of the things I had planned to say. But this is one of those days where right before I did my program or was planning to do my program. A very very heavy Spirit came over me to rebuke Israel. Now, this is something that I don't ever even recall doing in the past. It is a very grievous thing to do. In my opinion, it vexes my soul but as I was saying, this is one of those times where it was pretty heavy on me to obey and to speak these words that I am going to say with a heavy heart. I mean no harm. I feel led to do this. And so most Absolutely. Will I obey what I believe I have been given to say.

Now, anyone who listens to my radio programs, knows that one of the tenets of the things that I say has to do with whatever you do find a way to give glory to the God of Abraham, Isaac, and Jacob and also find a way to bear fruit any kind of way. Use your imagination. Take stock of yourself. Examine your gifts and abilities. Do not waste even one more second of time. Redeem the time. Work while it is day. Those brothers and sisters that you Israelites are sitting back and listening to… as they minister to you. And it bears no fruit of response in you. Those brothers and sisters are winning the kingdom. Now there is an event in Revelation chapter 14 It is called the wine press. And two thirds of you will experience it, you 1/3 of Hebrew Israelites who bear fruit, who do not let the world get in the way of finding somehow a way to minister or to be a light both now and in the eternal kingdom. The Heavenly Father has a plan to not let his word return void. For those of you nonresponding, Hebrew Israelites who are unable to respond to the good word of the Heavenly Father as it goes out. The Heavenly Father has a plan for you. I am talking to you nonresponding Hebrew Israelites. Those of you in my room who are listening to me in my room on Facebook you nonresponding brothers and sisters unable to respond to the word as it goes out. The Heavenly Father has a plan for you to get you to bear fruit for you, realm of matter, Israelites who care nothing about the God of Abraham, Isaac and Jacob who live for the world who love the world who are under Christianity and Catholicism that Heavenly Father has a plan for you who have not sought after the God of Abraham, Isaac and Jacob, who have not inquired after the God of Abraham Isaac and Jacob who have not sought or communed with the angels who do not give thanks for your daily bread. either before or after.

The Heavenly Father has a plan for you. His plan is the wine press of revelation 14 And you Israelites who bear no fruit who bear no response, who do not respond to His word to you the winepress is prepared. The Heavenly Father has a plan for you Hebrew Israelites who are unable to respond to action being a light. The Heavenly Father has a plan to extract his glory, His honor, out of those of you Hebrew Israelites who do not return his word with interest brothers and sisters my ministry is for Hebrew Israelites to give you hope and that is what I have tried to do these few years. I get very little return encouragement in return from you brothers and sisters. To which me personally I do not care.

But I realize I am an opportunity for you to do unto me as you would unto Messiah. Brothers and sisters, don't you understand? that as often as you do it to the least of these my brethren you have done it unto Messiah? So, when you are listening to me, and I am trying to encourage your soul your spirit to be motivated to bear fruit. And you do not even leave behind a thank offering. Not all of you. I have brethren who truly Bless my soul and I am not talking to you. But I testify based on experience I testify that the vast majority of you Hebrew Israelites who love to get off on what I say concerning you, and the good things are of the kingdom to come. Our future rulership. Us being given the desires of our heart freedom from captivity of our oppressors. Freedom to worship in my body, soul and spirit and everlasting peace. And joy, unending for an eternity. When I give you that message and you do not even leave in your wake a thank offering as witnessed by looking at my videos in the comment section. There is no response. There is no response to a brother trying his level best to minister to you. And there is no response.

Brethren, as often as you do it to me, you do it to Messiah, brethren for the last couple of weeks, I have shared a dream of a nationwide food ministry to minister to less fortunate Israelites who have a need of the basics of life, especially if they have children, I have asked for anyone who is willing to send me your city and state so that I may compile a list of brethren that I may call upon. In case there is a cry for charity that is coming out of our nation. I will not give up on that dream. until my last breath. But I want to share with you as of this date. Only one sister has volunteered to minister to anyone everywhere from the garden that she grows on her property… one… one sister.

Brethren, please. Often times I use earthly analogies to make my point if you show ingratitude to your spouse, what do you think will happen to you? That is one of the reasons for a relationship so that we may learn to be selfless to consider others, not just our self. America has taught us to be selfish to look after our own. To have an attitude of me first. Look out for number one. Get it while you can.

Brethren, we have truly been corrupted. I testify and I have been testifying that in order to receive you must give it doesn't always mean money. You can give of your company you can give your fellowship; you can give words of support. You can give a thank offering to any brother or sister who ministers to you. Messiah said My yoke is easy, and my burden is light, so therefore he does not ask you very much to show in return for the fact that he is gifted brethren to be able to minister unto you, to speak words unto you, to comfort you, to give you hope. Some brethren work some do not. I do not work. I am afflicted. I am handicapped for the time being. I am disabled and I prayed to be put in this position because it is easy for me to see the value in ministering the word of the God of Abraham, Isaac, and Jacob. It is easy for me to see the blessing and dedicating yourself as best you can to bearing fruit when the word goes out for your benefit but if the word goes out and produces in you, thorns and briers Brethren, this channel for one is not for you. And I beg also those who are listening, who are a part of my room on Facebook, who have been in my room for a little while now. There are nearly 40 of you brethren in my room and you bear no fruit other than to hit the like button or the emoji, but you will not do it to Messiah, but you will do it to a lowly brother like me. You will not do it to your spouse. But you will do it to a lowly brother such as myself.

Because you cannot see you cannot overstand that Messiah is using me to minister to you, yet you do not bear, you cannot bear any fruit of response. You do not overstand that Messiah was born in a manger. He was born in a lonely position. He took off his garment of glory. He laid it aside so people would not come to him for advantage. Brothers and sisters don't you understand that the Heavenly Father is using me to show you how thankful you are? Don't you realize that he is using me to expose the selfishness of your heart? Don't you remember the story of the 10 lepers and how they were all healed? And only one return to give glory to the point that Messiah asked the leper, where are the other nine? Messiah is showing you he wants you to respond to what he ministeres unto you. He gives you angels he gives you brethren; he gives you opportunity, but you are unable to respond.

Because you are sleeping. Brethren, I did not get a chance to speak prophetically. Tonight. Just before I came on the program, I came across an article stating that Nancy Pelosi has left for Asia. Now if you had been listening to me, or any other prophetical brothers, or watching the news you should know that the whole world is watching whether she will make the trip to Taiwan. Incidentally, my home is no more than 20 minutes from Nancy Pelosi's house. She is the Speaker of the House. China and the United States have gotten themselves into a position where neither one can back down. There is no way out. Whoever blinks first will be seen as weak. And the little itty bitty standing that America has left in the world. Will be greatly exposed and America will be seen as even weaker than what she already is now. Now I was going to talk a little about Evergrande Bank of China and the ramifications of its imminent default which will be felt around the world and suddenly we will be faced with the prospects of bank, failures of job loss, of an economic catastrophe, all because of this situation that you have not heard about. If they miss one more payment after already having missed two, we will feel it. There are many pots on the stove right now. And they are boiling hot and ready to boil over.

I'm sorry that I am able to elaborate. I've come to the end of my program.

Brethren, join me Wednesday and Friday. 8pm Pacific Standard Time on blog talk radio.

Join me and my brethren in my room on Facebook, the upper room. The link is in the description box on YouTube.

I want to give thanks to my Heavenly Father earthly mother for this incredible opportunity and until I see you again. peace be unto you

shalom

August July conflict

It is a funny thing that I am writing this book without even expecting it to make it to market. I honestly do not believe anyone will have a chance to read this particular book and still I am writing it and soon to finish it. I say this because of the current situation that has now arisen with Nancy Pelosi and the threat coming from China that if she visits Taiwan there will be a military response it is another event that has me truly shaking my head that this is really happening. There is no more alarm when nation governments speak of nuclear war. And now the situation has become very imminent that something must give, especially in this situation with Nancy Pelosi and her Taiwan visit and the Chinese government. By the time this book is published if it is published, the event will be over with and the conclusion known one way or another. It seems to me that this is how the God of Abraham Isaac and Jacob can blow a loud trumpet to warn the Hebrew Israelites who are looking diligently and searching anywhere they can find information concerning the restoration of the 12 tribes of Israel and return of Messiah. While keeping the rest of the nation oppressors totally oblivious to what is really going on spiritually through the events of the world. Although I must admit this is a pretty harrowing time when one considers the abilities of the Chinese to respond to any threat they perceive coming from America. There are a number of situations presently at hand that could go live spelling the end of this reality as we know it.

We have become like the proverbial frog in the boiling pot of water. All dangers have been slowly boiling to the point where they are now raging. No one knows which event will trigger the final conclusion of the white man's Kingdom, but we know without a shadow of a doubt the Negro, Latino and Native American Kingdom of the God of Abraham Isaac and Jacob to which the world says they want so badly is at hand. I do not believe they know what they are wishing for, because as I have observed this nation and Christianity, there is a high level of hypocrisy and ignorance when it comes to receiving the brutal truth about who the children of Israel are. But yet and still we are being shown through the confluence of events that we have now come to a point where the puzzle is nearly complete and the reality of the restoration of the children of Israel is manifesting in a very obvious way, to the incredible delight and overwhelming joy of the Israelites that know that we are in the final time of this current captivity of the oppressor nations who do not know that they are the oppressor nations of the Negro, Latino and Native American on their father's side.

I perceive that both America and the world (because of the current events which will undoubtedly trigger World War three) is facing a time when the biggest prayer meeting known to man will take place most likely to no avail since the time of repentance has long passed and the only thing this station and other oppressor nations can look forward to is recompense for the treatment of the children of Israel. I am amazed that I am actually writing things like this in a book. It is strictly for antiquity's sake.

Remove the oppressors power

 This is the Hebrew Israelite son flight radio program. I want to give thanks to my Heavenly Father earthly mother for this incredible opportunity to take my life and to use it to devote my energy and all that is within me to be a light shining towards glorifying thy heavenly father, the God of Abraham, Isaac and Jacob. This is a ministry for Hebrew Israelites you Negro, Latino and Native Americans. I have a room on Facebook for fellowship called the upper room. I am also an author; you can go to the links in my description box on YouTube to see the books that I've written I have another book that I will be finished with next week. You just go to Amazon and type in my name if you're interested and I try to write from a Hebrew Israelite perspective of my reality I have a website called twelvetribes Israelites all lowercase lettering spelled together. If anything, I say resonates with you. And you believe you want to get in touch with me you can just go to my website there. And you can send me a message. I also have a dream of a nationwide ministry in which anyone who may be suffering from food insecurities especially if you have children.

Why don't you contact me let me know so I can bring it before the nation in hopes that someone nearby can help to minister until you, the purpose of any ministry that I do is strictly to give you brethren and sisters hope and encouragement to draw nearer to the God of Abraham, Isaac and Jacob. I just hope that by my consistency over the years, that you will be able to see the power of the God of Abraham, Isaac, and Jacob to uphold a brother and to sustain a brother even though I am a disabled brother. I am a handicap brother I am not a rich brother. I hope that by looking at my example, that you will see the God of Abraham, Isaac and Jacob and how he has sustained me. Now, I named the title of the program tonight is "remove the oppressors power", remove the oppressors power. Now I want to start off by sharing a couple of stories with you. And matter of fact, this all happened in just a couple of days. Now I had to go to the hospital. And upon going to my appointment. I mentioned to the doctor that I had the chills and he wanted to send me to the emergency room because when you have chills It took me an infection. Now, I told him I didn't want to go I had no intention. of going to the emergency room. And before he could even answer a Hebrew sister jumped in and decided she was going to defend the doctor by scolding me like your mother would.

Now at this point, it took every fiber of my being not to raise up out of my power chair and squeeze her neck off of her body. I mean, I really was fired up over the sister sticking up for the doctor believing he needed to be defended. Now, it just so happens that I ran into her some months before in downtown San Francisco and I tried to explain to her who the Hebrew Israelites are. And I probably spent at least three hours trying to bless her with the knowledge that she belongs to an elite elect group of people she did not listen to one word. She has a forehead thicker than a mountain.

And so, I finally let the whole conversation go. Now, when I was in the doctor's office, she felt like she could lecture me on listening to what the doctor said because he's a good man and He cares for you. And that is why I wanted to squeeze her neck off of her body because Israelites can be like that. Messiah said there was going to tie there was going to be a time when men would not hear sound doctrine and that is especially the case today men will not hear sound doctrine. One thing that I have learned is that I must learn to remove the power of the oppressor to afflict me with thoughts of evil anger recompense. In other words, I learned the last couple of days. I must learn to be free and let the battle be the God of Abraham, Isaac and Jacob. Now this is not easy to do.

That is why when you read the Nag Hammadi. You will read about a realm that you Hebrew Israelites walking in the light walking in faith are surrounded by what is known as the beast Kingdom is referring to Israelites as well as the oppressor nations. These are people who have no spiritual inclination to hear sound doctrine are not willing and do not care. Now I want to share another story.

Coming home from the hospital. I ran into a neighbor of mine, and he was very badly shaken. And I asked him what is wrong? He said his son threatened to kill him and took the vehicle away from his dad and drove off at a high rate of speed with the neighbor's dog and the car. The father had refused to let this son have possession of the vehicle because he charged him with being irresponsible. And so, this son was living in the vehicle because he had no other place to go. Now, a few months earlier this is the same son who grabbed his father by the neck and was choking him and don't you know the very next day the son ended up in jail. And I saw an open door and I try to witness to the neighbor. Even if you do not believe in the God of Abraham, Isaac, and Jacob. There are times when his law are so flagrantly violated, that whether you are a child of Israel, or of the oppressor nations, the heavenly Father will step in and he will bring judgment to this situation And now, this situation where the Son has taken the car from his father and when I find out the conclusion, which I do not think will be a good one saying how this is the second time he has rebelled in this way against his father. The father may bring even more grievious judgment.

Now brothers and sisters, I'm sharing this with you because we live in a nation of young people and people in general who are becoming further and further removed from the fear of the God of Abraham, Isaac, and Jacob and I am referring to our people as well. Young people committing grievous acts of violence even against our own kind. I'm sure many of you know but I can testify I have seen instant judgment in my life too many times to know that it is real. One more story I will share that actually happened. Another neighbor of mine, a Hebrew was outside eating a plate of food. The food was pork, and he claimed to be a Muslim. And as I was going by, he wanted me to hear him say "I asked the Heavenly Father if I could eat poor just this one time. His response was the Heavenly Father who said I'll think about" it mocking God. I didn't laugh. And I went right by him even though he was expecting a response and don't you know two weeks later, he went to prison. So, I guess the heavenly father fought it over and decided to send him off for a little stripe sunshine. To which he is still looking at today almost two years later,

Brethren we are living in a time where people will learn the fear of the God of Abraham Isaac and Jacob. The Heavenly Father promises that. One of the lessons that I learned as well, these past couple of days is that we must free ourselves from the power of the oppressor.

Now, going back to my hospital stay I let the doctor talk me in to being admitted. And I told the various doctors that came to speak with me that I did not want to be admitted. And they begin to speak all kinds of death over me. And a thought came to my mind I had to break their power to vex me like that. And so, they threatened me with possibly dying, which is their favorite. Go to and threatened me with physical maladies and illnesses which is another one of their favorite go to warnings. And so, for as many doctors that I talked to the Spirit gave me the wisdom to take their power away. The common denominator of the physicians that talk to me was Aren't you afraid that you could die? And to each one I said no. But if I were you, I would be afraid to die. And when they saw that they had no more power over me that their power was taken away by me. Then they begin to back off. And a couple of doctors began to reason with me why I was so hard on the medical profession. So, I began to share with them. I know about aliopathic medicine. I know that previous to its ascent to where it has evolved into pharmaceutical, American Medical Association. Previous to the advent of modern-day medicine, natural medicine was the norm for treatment of illnesses. And wounds. But when John Rockefeller saw that you could make scientific medicine using petroleum. He began to establish universities with the stipulation only allopathic medicine could be taught even back then.

He saw profit and cancer rates began to skyrocket all because of profit and greed. And that is why alternative medicine, natural medicine. Organic medicine fell by the wayside. So, we have what we have today And I'm saying only for myself, because we are not all strong enough. To get rid alopathic medicine, including myself. Although I have done away with the nearly 15 pills, I was supposed to take on a daily basis down to three many brethren, not strong enough to do things like that. And I for one, overstand that but I found an incredible amount of freedom when I took those doctors and nurses assistants power away from them. And I put my trust in the God of Abraham, Isaac and Jacob. He gave me an anointing to take their power away.

They were confused. They were baffled as I begin to tell them about the real reason for the vaccinations and the different depopulation agendas that we are currently under and the education that they received, where it started, what the purpose of it was and that they are on the wrong side of history for not holding to the Scripture in the Apocrypha that tells us that medicine was made is made out of the earth

Brethren we must remove the power over the oppressors. We must not love the world. We must look forward to the eternal kingdom. The Heavenly Father has not given us the spirit of fear. But of power and a sound mind. The nations do not overstand this because they do not know the God of Abraham and Jacob. This mindset is sure to make you solitary in the world. Messiah said blessed are the elect and solitary for

They Will find the kingdom brethren, let me share this with you, manna or the word is food, which we must eat of. The beauty of the gospel is you can flavor your food whatever way you like, in order to benefit you and to increase you and your overstand there are many gifted brethren in our nation whose fruit you can eat to have in order to bear fruit and increase and grow. We are living in a time where we if you are watching are certainly going to see a change in our reality. Did you know that there is another hotspot in the world between Serbia and Kosovo? right over there in the area of south of the Ukraine. We are in a time where there are boiling pots all ready to boil over. The time escapes me. I want to say if anyone under the sound of my voice and would like to have fellowship with me and my brethren click on the link in my YouTube description box. And come and have fellowship and let me encourage you to continue in the faith and to store up for yourself and to redeem the time and to remove the oppressors power which for many holds us captive to the fear of death all our lives.

I want to give thanks to my Heavenly Father earthly mother for this incredible opportunity.

Please join me Wednesday and 5pm Pacific Standard Time and until I meet with you again.

peace be unto you Shalom

YOUR KINGDOM OUR KINGDOM

I want to give thanks to my Heavenly Father earthly mother for this incredible opportunity that they give me every Wednesday and Friday 8pm Pacific Standard trying to try to be a light while I am in this reality. Absolutely. Without question. The greatest opportunity known to man is to be a Hebrew Israelite. Who is seeking to be a light and to draw near to the God of Abraham, Isaac and Jacob there is no comparison to the opportunity that the Hebrew Israelites have in this current reality.

Now, this is a ministry for Hebrew Israelites. I have a room on Facebook for fellowship called the upper room. In addition, I am an author I write books. I will be finished with my next book. In a few days, you can go to Amazon and type in my name and my books should come up. I have a website called twelvetribesisraelites.com all spelled together lowercase lettering where you can get in touch with me in case I'd say anything that resonates with you. I also have a dream of a nationwide ministry for the Hebrew Israelites for the purpose of ministering to the less fortunate of us who may have a food need especially if you have children. I would like to get in contact with you or I would like someone to put me in contact with someone. And I would like to bring the issue before the nation to see if a brother or sister nearby can minister to the struggling brother or sister contact me at twelvetribes israelites.com.

Now I also hope to be an encouragement. I want to be an encouragement for my nation. I want to help anyone simply to be focused and to try your level best not to lose faith, to remember the God of Abraham, Isaac and Jacob to try to help you know the things that are lined up against you in the world that you will not hear about in the mainstream media. I try to inform you of secret agendas like the current depopulation program of the vaccinations. And that reminds me I have been suspended from YouTube if anyone listens to me on YouTube I have been suspended for two weeks. I started out with a warning on my channel and I went from warning to two strikes. So, I will not be doing videos on YouTube. If anyone is listening. I will be doing my programs on platforms like this one. Or on my Facebook page where you can hear my live programs.

Now I entitle the name of the program tonight. "Your kingdom our kingdom". Now, presently the confluence of events in the world from my perspective, only mean one thing. The kingdom of the white man and the people who say they are Jews and are not is drawing to a conclusion. The Asiatic nations are forming their own alliances, establishing their own trading bloc's beginning to do business with themselves and excluding Europe and the United States. From my perspective, the United States does not want to lose its position as the preeminent power in the world. When you look at history, every so many years, power goes from the east. Then after so many years, it goes to the west. And then another 500 years later, it goes back to the east. And that is where we are right now. Power is transitioning to the east, primarily to Russia and China. And there is nothing America can do about it. The confluence of events can only lead to one conclusion and that is nuclear war, for someone such as myself, seeing the food shortages, the orchestrated food shortages, the situation with Revelation chapter six, first three. The current vaccination depopulation program the hostilities that are brewing and are ongoing such as Russia, and China. All these things were predicted by the project that I mentioned a few months back on my video telling you about "project Looking Glass" when it foresaw the current events and what they must lead to. What they will lead to, if there is any Hebrew Israelite listening to the sound of my voice, you should take courage. You should take heart you should realize this is the God of Abraham, Isaac, and Jacob telling you that we are fast running out of time to build a testimony to be a light to prepare for the eternal kingdom. The nations they know their kingdom is coming to an end they do not want to admit it. Especially America when I looked at social media, they do not give glory to the God of Abraham, Isaac and Jacob. They give glory to the dollar to gold and silver. They give more glory to their guns. They give glory to the military. They will not reason amongst themselves, why these things are coming upon them. Why every move America makes backfire backfires on them. They do not consider they do not inquire about the God of Abraham, Isaac and Jacob. And for such a one as myself. I could not be happier because I know this these events and other events that I have not mentioned. Show me that our kingdom is on the horizon.

Now I recall seeing a story of a slave woman who did not want her child to grow up in slavery. She threw her child into the river, when I heard that story I had no more tears to cry because I had run out of tears for my nation a long time ago. I am all dried up inside. It only fueled my desire to look diligently for any shred of information of when we will leave this damnable white man, fake Jew reality. And I began to consider the differences between our kingdom and their kingdom and thought came to my mind there is a big difference. A very big, moral spiritual difference in the Hebrew Israelite kingdom and the current kingdom of Amalek, Esau and Japheth now, if I may I would like to relate another story before I go into the contrasting kingdoms.

A neighbor of mine where I live shared with me the story of his wayward son. And as it turns out, his son had nowhere to go and was sleeping in his father's car. Because he was banned from the property where his father, my neighbor lives. So, he stayed in the vehicle for maybe three weeks. Until the other day where he violently ripped the keys out of his father's hand. And he took the car that he was using to sleep in and is now on the run. Now, the neighbor told me the father of the son related to me how disrespectful his son is towards him and how he fears for his life now, because his son already choked him one time, I mentioned this a few weeks back on one of my videos that I tried to witness to my neighbor. One of the ways you can see the Heavenly Father is by the judgment he brings when he steps in from time to time. But I digress in this kingdom you can grab your mom and dad in this kingdom. You can cuss out your mom and dad. I recall living next to an Ito mine who had a wayward son. And even though her son must have been only five, four or five years old he would talk back to her liike she was a child. You see in this kingdom you can disrespect your parents.

Now, I'm not speaking of an Israelite kingdom in our kingdom even today I remember being knocked out by my dad when I did not clean the bathroom to his liking. And I have heard similar stories of Hebrew fathers administering discipline. I never witnessed Hebrew child an Israelite speaking back to his mom or dad and not suffer brutal consequences. But in this kingdom, you can be a kid and boss your parents around. In this kingdom the oppressor they can shoot us in the city. They can shoot us and the country. They can defraud us of our wages in this kingdom they can make treaties with you and break them. Go ahead and ask the Native Americans what I am talking about, in this kingdom where we live you can lie right to someone's face and tell them how healthy and safe this vaccination is. In this kingdom you can take a shower with your daughter as a grown man, you could take a shower with your daughter, and you can become President of the United States. Go ahead. Just ask Joe Biden. In this country here you can be caught on tape talking about how you like to violate women know just kind of grab them right there. And you know what? You can be elected president of the United States, in this country in this kingdom the law goes for you, Israelites not for our oppressors. In this kingdom. You can blaspheme the God of Abraham, Isaac, and Jacob. You can curse his name in this kingdom. You can rob other people of their resources the Africans should know what I am talking about. And there is nothing they can do about it. In this kingdom, they can charge you usury in this kingdom. In this kingdom you can do all the drugs you can get your hands on in this kingdom.

This is a kingdom that feeds on the death industry. Consciously through agendas and secret programs to decrease the size of people so the elite can have more and more and more, and you Israelites have less and less and less, in our kingdom the oppressor shall come bending unto the Hebrew Israelite. They will come bending and bowing to us in the city. They will come bending and bowing to us in the country. They will cling to our garments and our kingdom in the Hebrew Israelite kingdom and our kingdom there will be no lie, in our kingdom we will suck the milk of the Gentiles in our kingdom and our kingdom. Our Father will be a loving father but to the nation's a stern King. In our kingdom, the Hebrew Israelites will sing for joy of heart for ever. Going out into the field with seed and coming home shouting with a harvest in our kingdom. In our kingdom, never again will we know the whip in our kingdom the oppressors for them, the whip will not cease until they are destroyed, in our kingdom there will be justice in our kingdom, there will be the knowledge of God. The God of Abraham Isaac and Jacob and our kingdom. There will be no more talk of politics and money and silver and gold and prepping and underground bunkers and nuclear bombs. In our kingdom there will be no more pedophilia. There will be no more Satan in the kingdom of the God of Abraham and Isaac and Jacob. The creation will shout for joy at the manifestation of the sons of God restored in spiritual power fulfilling Ezekiel chapter 12 Verse 14 recompensing our enemies and then after we are done 1000 years later, then and may be then in our kingdom. We can be a brother hood of men, in our kingdom in our kingdom, the Israelite prisoner will go free in the eternal kingdom in the God of Abraham, Isaac, and Jacob when the children of Israel currently in captivity will sang everlasting praise because of the abundance of all things in our kingdom. There will be no censorship. There will be no hiding the truth there will be no abortion. There will be no upside down order of the family in our kingdom, the coming Kingdom the Kingdom of the children of Israel that the world does not want to know about but they see us coming and they hide their heads in the sand even deeper and live in the river of denial because there's nothing they can do. And so, with each passing day, as we draw closer to the winter to the elections to Europe freezing to death because of the sanctions Russia puts on them as we get closer to Pluto completing its death rebirth cycle and the" x" over America there is nothing the nations can do.

 Thank you for joining me I want to give thanks my Heavenly Father Earthly mother for this incredible opportunity.

Join me Wednesday and Friday, pm Pacific Standard Time until I see you again.

Peace to unto you

shalom

A DREAM

it is a dream
It is my dream
It will come to pass
It will come to pass

Eternal in nature
Restored old friendships
Renewed family acquaintances
It is a dream

But at the same time
It is reality
Ultimate reality
Perfection of all things

It does exist
Let all tongues confess
Maybe not now
But they will

It is a dream
And then it is not
It is foretelling
The new Kingdom

When with this test
We are finished
Then and only then
My writing pen

Will rest

From having to
Recount
The failure of man
To achieve rest

It is a dream

A dream of mine
The justice I dream of
Most certainly will be
Realized

Everyone I know
By my side

Who blessed my soul
In this life
Smiling and laughing
Not afraid to give thanks

Not afraid to say
I love the God of
Abraham Isaac and Jacob
As they are now

It is a dream of mine
And this dream
Will come to pass
With my eyes

I shall behold it
And others will too
But they will mourn
Because

Their dream now
Over
Abundance of gold
And silver no more

A temporary dream
Instead of eternal reality
Makes no sense
To me

But my dream
It is my dream

And I paid a price
To overcome ...

Forsaking the world
And its promises
of wealth

Using slavery
Deception
Robbery
Through corruption

Of character

It was a dream
For this reality
For which
Many did receive

Not believing
Anything better
Could ever be
But I knew

In my soul
My dream
It is my dream
Greater than all

Lil nutshell

To live
Is a righteous thing
To give
When someone

 is in need

Makes life
Worth living
When because
Of you

They bless his name

This life
Is a temporary test
What way
Will ye go?

Suffering and affliction
Or self-serving
What will ye do?
When all said and done?

This is
The nutshell
On which the future
Depends

Will you be counted
With the overcomers?
Easily choosing
Suffering and affliction

Because
It looks like Messiah?
Pointing the way
On the road we are on

So, let's follow it

Bottoms up August 2022

War with China looks guaranteed any day now. China has been holding
live fire drills and even has installed a blockade around Taiwan. All
because (In my opinion) the United States must go to war with Russia
and China and the plan to send Nancy Pelosi to Taiwan will help
accomplish just that (at least with Taiwan). Even if nothing does happen,
I find I am really getting very weary of living in the white man's
Kingdom and the fake Jews. All they have shown us in the previous
generations is agendas and secret plans for world domination and
population control. I know I feel like the multitude of people in the
world today who are simply just trying to live from day-to-day. I
happen to live in a place where the men seem to have figured out how
to deal with the constant flood of news of one dangerous situation after
another. They spend their days drinking and numbing themselves to
the confluence of events going on around them. They are thoroughly
preoccupied only with feeding their head with the world of escapism.
To be honest I cannot blame them, they want some sort of relief from
what they must know in the back of their mind is true. Which is at some
point there will be a global conflict the likes of which we have never
seen before and there is no solution in sight. I would imagine that
across the nation people who own liquor stores are getting rich. I would
not be surprised to know that the political leaders have stock in liquor
sales. The human condition is a sad sight to see at least in my reality as
people are willing to live on the lowest basic animal level from day-to-
day. If I were to be honest, I would say without any foundation in the
God of Abraham Isaac or Jacob this cannot be what living was meant to
be. I feel sorry for the vast majority of people I see. I know right now,
they probably feel sorry for me.

UNFAIR

I heard someone say
Life is not fair
That is true
Spiritually

For spiritual people
For the Hebrew
The children of Israel
The Negro

Indeed
Life is not fair
Has to be that way
Blessing and curse

They go together
The sons of light
An awesome price
Is tendered

It must be paid
The length of life
The decree
Set from all high

In order to gain
The precious by
And by

But for now
Life is not fair

So, that when
The sons and daughters
Enter the heavenly realm
Life then

No longer unfair

Or wait a moment
Life will be unfair
For the unbelieving
For the untested

For the apathetic
Indeed, it is true
Life will be unfair

When the sons and daughters
Of the Hebrew Messiah
Go about
In the land

With praise and shout
Because
they believed
In that which

could not
Be seen

In this earthly
Reality
And they endured
In pain and tears

To find that city
On a hill
Filled with
All good things

To which access
They will have
In a way like
No other

Who have trodden
The lonely path

In suffering
But in faith

Now rejoicing
Because of
The abundance
Of all things

It is true
Life is unfair
You see
It had to be

That way

The choice is ours
Our life is
What decides
Which side of unfair

We eternally reside

CELEBRATION

One day
While watching TV
While watching
The championships

Of the elite
One thing
Was common
Human joy

Expressed
And the fullest
Very infectious
Spreading to one
Spreading to all

As the victor
Overcomes
All odds
The crown

On his head
Is placed
Hands are clapping
There is shouting

The victor
Nose sweet joy
The struggle
Crushing solitariness

As they went about
Waiting for
The peak moment
To perform

So therefore
The time came

All his effort
All his training
In hopes of
Joy to bring
To his body
To his soul

To his spirit
That few of us
Can know
To achieve

And to experience
And overwhelming sense
To touch
The finger of God

When all
Is said
When all
Is done

And the people
Cheered greatly
Even if
Vicariously

At the accomplishments
Of the athlete
In the Colosseum
Exhibiting his skills

Herculean feats
Overcoming in life
Many at times
Experiencing defeat

So that when
He overcomes
The victory won

Never can his joy

Keep from
Uplifting
All men
From the current reality

Of the temporary
Pain of suffering
It is the gift
Of the God

Of Abraham
Of Isaac
Of Jacob

HALALYAH

Mom

Well mom I did it it's hard for me to believe I am even saying this seeing how much I hated school as I'm sure you will know. I am now finished with my sixth book. I love remembering you by way of writing I love using the example of your life, you showed me while you were here to form my perspective that I now carry. Mom, I love you for your abilities and the faults that you showed me and the genuineness of human character and how beautiful and has no price comparable to it. That is what I miss the most about you is your genuine original character and how you were not afraid of hard work has most Capricorns are not. You gave me a gift that is sustaining me all my life which is to believe and to work for what I believe in. The world is a dangerous place right now and I know I will be reunited with you very shortly and I cannot wait to see all of you in the restored Hebrew Kingdom. I am estranged from Chuck the vibration between us has become too great to overcome. It can be overcome but now the time is too short, and the effort needed to overcome the vibration is too great for me. I will to get him back in the eternal kingdom. But for right now, I have to use all my energy to run to the God of Abraham Isaac and Jacob so that perhaps I may be accounted worthy to escape the things coming on the earth. I know you are proud of me mom for trying to do what is right by my life. Doing what is right in a man was always the most important thing to you meaning to be responsible and to help other people. T[his was your character and because of it I will know no greater love than the one I have for you.

Until I see you again
Peace be unto you mom
Shalom

DAD

Well dad I am now finished with my 6th book. I can just imagine the look on your face if I had told you when I was younger I was going to write books. But I know that you would have always believed in me and I know that you are proud of my efforts to do what is right by my life and to share about my God the best way I know how. Remember the time I interviewed you on my camcorder? And I asked you who you liked as president and you said Joe Biden. Dad I am sorry to say that he has been an absolute disaster and is probably hands down the worst president this country has ever known. He is involved with influence peddling graft and he has a son who is a drug addict and is being accused of relations with underage children. The president himself is also accused of pedophilia something I know would burn your soul if you knew of such things in a person. I am estranged from Chuck because the vibration between the both of us is too great I have to wait until the eternal Kingdom to get him back. But like I was telling mom I have to use all my energy to run for my life to the God of Abraham Isaac and Jacob and that is what I am doing. The world is a very very perilous place right now I'm glad you and mom do not have to experience what is going on in this reality. I know that I will see you very soon. I think of you often and give thanks for the things that you have shown me through my spirit through your spirit. A lot of people are picking the Cincinnati Bengals to win it this year.

And until I see you again
peace be unto you dad
Shalom